Sana, Sana

ADVANCE PRAISE

"Praise forever to the warrior healers who transform the world by opening their hearts. This anthology models the self-compassion that we need to live as our complex evolving selves. These writers are now my teachers for life. May we understand our healing as creation, reclamation, and multi-generational love. This book is here to bless you in all directions."
—**Alexis Pauline Gumbs**, PhD, author of *Undrowned: Black Feminist Lessons from Marine Mammals* and *Dub: Finding Ceremony*

"With *Sana, Sana: Latinx Pain and Radical Visions for Healing and Justice*, editors David Luis Glisch-Sánchez and Nic Rodríguez Villafañe have ushered forth a timely, biting anthology of Latinx perspectives on contemporary social and historical culture; as the social and the historical are framed by settler colonialism, capitalism, the violence of individual and collective trauma, antihuman phobias and other structures of dominance. The question raised here, grounded in Latinx, feminist and queer thought, in the idea that 'healing requires witness,' is, simply put, how can those of us who have been harmed intergenerationally and across worlds, across time, create and define what we mean by reparation(s). *Sana, Sana* arrives at a critical moment in twenty-first century abolitionist practice."
—**Alexis De Veaux**, author of *JesusDevil: The Parables*

"*Sana, Sana* is a transformative anthology that mixes raw emotions, trauma, self-awareness, politics, spirituality, and sometimes even humor. Shared narratives of pain and collective transformation are expressed through poetry, storytelling, and testimonios, envisioning a different kind of world. It is a manual for Latinx hope."
—**Lawrence La Fountain-Stokes**, author of *Translocas: The Politics of Puerto Rican Drag and Trans Performance*

"First you have to name it. Say it. Unearth it. Then stomp it. And scream. Twirl it. Open to the Sky and howl it. Cry. Step into the Circle. It's ritual. Sacred Openings that beckon us to dance and laugh and Love and feel and heal anyway. This is what *Sana, Sana* gives us. Mirrors. Pathways. Shimmering Light. All of this and so much more. Now is the perfect time to read this book. And Receive."
—**Sharon Bridgforth**, writer, performing artist, and author of *bull-jean & dem/dey back*

"Without apology, the voices in this anthology reveal the complexities of living with pain while simultaneously pursuing healing and justice. Whether exploring the intersections of race, gender, sexuality, or class, these works remind us that we are never alone in our pain and do not have to be alone in our healing. These stories are rooted in the power of community, connection—and ultimately love. *Sana, Sana* demonstrates that we all have healing tools at our disposal whether that be music, prayer, Vicks VapoRub, sewing, or simply taking shots with a friend over Facetime. The poems and essays in this collection define the reclamation of our power to heal ourselves and our communities as holy work. This work is necessary, bold, unflinching, and a timely addition to contemporary Latinx literature."
—**Elisabet Velasquez**, author of *When We Make It: A Nuyorican Novel*

ISBN: 978-1-942173-78-6 | eBook ISBN: 978-1-942173-94-6
Library of Congress Number: 2023938225
10 9 8 7 6 5 4 3 2 1

Common Notions
c/o Interference Archive
314 7th St.
Brooklyn, NY 11215

Common Notions
c/o Making Worlds Bookstore
210 S. 45th St.
Philadelphia, PA 19104

www.commonnotions.org
info@commonnotions.org

Discounted bulk quantities of our books are available for organizing, educational, or fundraising purposes. Please contact Common Notions at the address above for more information.

Cover design by Josh MacPhee
Layout design and typesetting by Graciela "Chela" Vasquez | ChelitasDesign
Printed by union labor in Canada on acid-free paper

Sana, Sana
Latinx Pain and Radical Visions
for Healing and Justice

David Luis Glisch-Sánchez and
Nic Rodríguez-Villafañe, editors

Brooklyn, NY
Philadelphia, PA
commonnotions.org

Table of Contents

Introduction

David Luis Glisch-Sánchez & Nic Rodríguez Villafañe

Queridx:

Thank you for witnessing. As a sacred part of healing, witnessing allows us to see ourselves as whole and healthy—an act of pure rebellion in a world so titillated by our constant subjugation and conquest. We hope that you find that this anthology listens as well as poses questions and strives for answers. And just when we seem to find the rhythm of peace, something else arises. Healing is not linear. Each voice in this anthology uses the pages to *desahogar*, a direct translation says to vent, but the literal meaning is to undrown. Here in this anthology, you will find writers who release that which keeps their throats on fire. Letting go of secrets and burdens, unraveling our *papelitos guardados*.[1] May we no longer drown from the memories of pain left unsaid. As many have experienced trauma, our instinct is to silence ourselves, to swallow our pain. We know this is one way why generational legacies of trauma continue to exist. What if the one way to interrupt this legacy of pain, is to begin with the honest sharing of our stories?

The idea for *Sana, Sana* was birthed from the experiences that David (coeditor) had in interviewing queer and trans Latinxs about their encounters with social harm and learning the narratives they created and responded to around pain, trauma, and healing. In the dozens of hours of recorded conversations, it was clear: Latinx folx not only had a lot to say about pain and heal-

---

1 We draw on the idea of *papelitos guardados* as presented by The Latina Feminist Group in *Telling to Live: Latina Feminist Testimonios* (Duke University Press, 2001). They write, "*Papelitos guardados* evokes a process by which we contemplate thoughts and feelings, often in isolation and through difficult times. We keep them in our memory, write them down, and store them in safe places waiting for the appropriate moment when we can return to them for review and analysis, or speak out and share them with others."

ing, but each, in their own way, *yearned* to talk about, share, and express these hard truths. Although the method was collaborative, this initial project was singularly driven and conceived of by David. All the while the collective need that was expressed repeatedly in the process was simply that Latinx folx needed their own space where a multitude of voices, testimonios, and knowledges could be expressed, heard, and engaged with. An anthology seemed like the most appropriate vehicle to hold and nurture this need.

From the beginning, it was apparent that this effort required more than one pair of guiding hands. Nic's experience as an organizer, gifts as a poet, calling as a healer, and depth as an intellectual made them an ideal and desired coconspirator and collaborator. Unbeknownst to David at the time, Nic was wrestling with some of the very same questions that would become the core of this anthology. It would seem the Universe had plans for us all along. We share the genesis of this project to articulate and underscore the fact that this anthology is more than just a book filled with pages of writing. Rather, it is best understood as ritual, ceremony, and technology—an invitation to enter your individual and our collective wounds communally. Through our writing, your reading, and the multitude of exchanges that undoubtedly will transpire, we catalyze our healing and call forth visions of and roadmaps for justice.

The project was introduced to the wider public via social media in January 2021, and within hours, hundreds of people had begun to share the call for submissions. During a time when so many of us were in isolation (almost a year into the COVID-19 pandemic) and hungry for connection, the call for this anthology served as a bridge for folks to share stories and histories and parts of their pain and healing. In this age we find ourselves, so many are searching to find a true set of customs that belong rightfully to self. In this time of feeling lost in the braided storylines of conqueror and conquered, it might just be that participating together in the ritual of storytelling is the most fundamental act of living. In reclaiming this birthright, we take back our humanity. It is about saying and doing what we need/want to imagine and heal. Each voice in this anthology offers a space to talk and feel pain, while also offering the hope of what it means to imagine, heal, and make promises to and for a more just world.

We take as our title, the beginning words of the popular Latinx, Caribbean, and Latin American children's folk saying "Sana,

sana colita de rana ponte buena para mañana . . . ,"[2] a common refrain given to children when they get hurt. In fact, the opening words "Sana, sana" provide a calm but firm command to heal. The saying operates as an emotional and spiritual salve to reassure the hurt child that despite whatever pain they might be feeling and experiencing in that moment, healing is a technology and process that is open and available to them. In this same way, it is our intention that the anthology be a reminder to all people that healing is not a commodity for the few, but a resource for all, and that justice is just another name for healing the collective body.

The anthology is divided into three general themes. It can be read from beginning to end, or as individual sections. As a reader you have the freedom to choose which section feels most aligned with your own present journey.

PAIN: SPEAKING THAT WHICH WANTS TO REMAIN UNSPOKEN

Pain is the word we give to a constellation of emotions and feelings that at their root are trying to communicate one thing: all is not well. Pain, whether collectively felt or individually experienced, is an invitation for change, a call for addressing harm, a demand for bringing into balance that which is out of it. Pain in its most understood form is physical, usually associated with some form of injury, illness, or disease; however, it more often than not manifests itself emotionally, psychologically, and spiritually. The pieces in this section wrestle with this multidimensional nature of pain, leaving us with the overarching message that Latinx pain must be expressed, must be named, must be acknowledged. In some of the most poignant pieces we learn that the words we choose to use to describe our pain are hard earned and often require us to evolve or create our own languages to capture the enormity of it.

Through poetry, fiction, memoir, and creative nonfiction, we come to observe that Latinx pain is a wide-branched tree with many deep and varied roots. We see how systemic forms of white supremacy, settler colonialism, misogyny, hetero- and

2 The folk saying as written here is how it was communicated within David's Cubanx familia. We recognize that each region, country, island, and family might have slight variations, but all begin with the words "Sana, sana colito de rana . . . " whose intent and purpose is similar, if not identical.

cis-normativity, and global capitalism have created the context and provided the source material for the violence and traumas affecting Latinx people. Pain often lives for people in the constantly negotiated distances between community and self, safety and silence, or acceptance and complicity. Aja Y. Martinez's memoir essay, "Counterstory as Catharsis: Alejandra's Deepest Wound," vividly showcases how deeply etched familial trauma is experienced and that only through the physical act of writing, the author could begin to untangle the memory of hurt. In different flashbacks, Martinez time hops through the multidimensional space a wound can occupy. In remembering, we may see the wound, and in retelling the memory we may encounter catharsis.

We also see that Latinx pain has not only been sourced from the outside, but also from within. That, as Audre Lorde warned, we have taken the master's tools to create our own houses of harm and terror. As examples, the poems of Lysz Flo, "How to tell my Novio, Mama, Abuela"—reflect on and depict the all too long history of internalized white supremacy in the forms of anti-Black racism and colorism. Corrosive forces that have eaten away at the bonds of family and community.

It is our hope that through the unflinching gaze of all the contributors' work, a reckoning will occur in the mind, heart, and spirit of you, that at last allows us to take a firm hold of our individual and collective pain and understand the many complex truths that result if and when we do.

HEALING: MAKING OURSELVES WHOLE

If we start with the proposition that healing is the process of making ourselves whole or remembering our wholeness to begin with, then the authors whose pieces appear in this section of the anthology remind us of the everyday resources and intergenerational traditions we have access to that can nurture, support, and guide our healing. Healing is a birthright for all humanity, not the commodity or experience of a special few. The ideas and lessons found in these works ask us to consider how dominant ideologies of race, gender, sexuality, class, ability, and spirituality have colonized our very understanding of what healing is, should look like, and how it needs to unfold.

Sinai Cota's poem "La Leyenda del Vaporu/The Legend of Vaporub" uses memory to conjure hope: ". . . I'd dream of her healing hands, warm, trying to make me feel better at night as my airway struggled to supply enough oxygen to my brain." Many readers will resonate with Cota's illustration of this childhood staple of healing, found in the medicine cabinets of many Latinx households. Whether the tools and practices we reach for take the form of a loving friendship, a cherished childhood memory, working with our multitudes of ancestor helping spirits, sacred ceremonies and rituals that pre-date the imposition of Christianity over our African and Indigenous cosmologies, or the hypnotic rhythm of music that dresses our wounds, we come to realize that healing is found in the ordinary and not the extraordinary.

Our everyday lived experiences are a cultural expression of magic. Raquel Reichard's "How Latin Trap Helped Me Heal from the Biggest Romantic Heartbreak of my Life" illustrates a type of mysticism in healing that happens in the surrender of our sounds. Reichard reminds us that the expression of reggaeton and Latin trap, "musica urbana," the underground, a genre historically imbued in controversy over its sexual and explicit content—is at its core—the most expressive of human experience. Reichard allows us to be part of her healing from heartbreak, a most intimate wound. In reggaeton/Latin trap she finds not only transmutation, but transformation:

> These frequent reggaeton parties aren't mending my broken heart alone—my ongoing self-awareness and self-care practices are doing most of that work—but they are helping me regain a confidence in myself that I thought was gone forever and allowing me to discover a sexy that I never even knew existed. *Pero tú 'ta grande, 'ta madura/Pasan los años y te pones más dura* I take a sip of champagne between laughs as Bad Bunny sings through a speaker in my hotel room, where I celebrated my 28th birthday last July.

Reichard illustrates this kaleidoscopic process of heartbreak, recovery, and rediscovery, through a cherished youthful expression of music and dance. Perreo has shown itself to be the music of revolution, the anthem of young Puerto Ricans during the uprisings of summer 2019, where thousands of Puerto Ricans demanded the Governor resign (he did). The expansive possibilities of the genre of music can be seen in Reichard's essay, where she reminds us that healing can only take place in the present, not the past, evoking a sort of future world making for our individual and collective selves.

These pieces and all the others that populate this section demand we recognize both our innate capacity for healing and the intuitive knowing we possess that outlines the specific ingredients for our own restorative journeys. They hint at the fact that individual healing is only a prelude to collective reparation, and that healing is an absolute requirement for justice.

JUSTICE: DEFIANT WORLDMAKING

Building on the provocations of the first two sections, authors here wrestle with the relationship between healing and justice, and its many individual and collective manifestations. We posit that one of the central themes or messages that runs through most, if not all, of the pieces in this section is the notion that justice, at its core, is a form of defiant worldmaking. Justice are those macro-social shifts and micro-social tactics that confront, disassemble, and abandon beliefs and practices that replicate and maintain current destructive forces in favor of creatively new and lifegiving paradigms and ways of being. These efforts are carried out in the face of logics that continuously counsel that it cannot be done; that justice is a utopia that exists just beyond the horizons of our perceptions and understandings. Grounding our understanding of justice in this way raises many politically pragmatic questions: Why do healers get separated outside of strategy in liberation ideas? Why are healers not at certain movement tables? Why don't we center healing as a political strategy in liberation struggles? Healing should be an extension of any political and social justice work. Our writers in this section provide us plans, visions, and dreams of the possibility of the worlds we can create.

This is the counsel that many healing justice advocates are offering. Our movement spaces are exhausted. Too many folks try to do all of their healing work while in a specific movement space, event or meeting—and oftentimes inadvertently perpetuate the same harms of the many oppressive systems our movements are fighting to eradicate. Healing is difficult to envision when our systems of care are rooted in the medical industrial complex; a western model of care, in which corporations exploit the health of patients and control the access to care by profiting from medical supplies and resources. Justice demands that we eradicate all systems of harm and create new ways of being. Justice means we have the limitless possibilities of imagining new ways of caring for each other, and our health. In order to do that, it is imperative we have space to navigate our own wounds and journey of restoration. We hope this anthology provides some of that space.

It is important to note and recognize that of the three major themes—pain, healing, and justice— it was justice that received the least amount of attention and engagement from prospective submissions. We believe this is indicative of the real challenge everyday folks have envisioning and birthing new modes of being that make a complete break with the legacies of harm and violence and that center a real and systemic love of humanity. It is this very real difficulty and challenge that this section attempts to speak to and become the impetus for all of us to become defiant worldmakers in the service of love and life.

You will find pieces in this section that stir the desire for creation and rebirth. Edyka Chilomé, in "A Recommendation," reminds us that we must first look at ourselves:

> . . . call in the magic buried in your blood
> dare to break open in climax by your own hands
> for our work now is to bloom beautiful in chaos
> and return home come winter

Chilomé confronts that we must give into the daily practices of self-preservation; loving and caring for ourselves in moments of self-intimacy that are creatively new and life giving, reminding us of the power of pleasure. Invoking Lorde's "power of the erotic" these practices of self-desire and love make possibilities seem real. In conversation with Edyka's poem, the essay "'Do you see me?': Musings on the Pain of Anti-Black Denial/Rejection in Latinx Spaces" by Biany Pérez also invokes the teachings of Lorde. Pérez proclaims power in being both "insider" and "outsider." At one point, Pérez sings to us a litany of what justice is:

> . . . Justice work is knowing ourselves
> Justice work is embracing our differences
> Justice work is embodying difficult truths. . .

We reject the notion that justice is an impossible dream or an eternal longing never to be fulfilled. The authors create a collective invitation for you, to connect with your own inner chingonx and bring that defiant energy to not only refuse the disciplining and colonizing forces of white supremacy, misogyny, hetero- and cis-normativity, and capitalism, but to marshal the courage to commit to new and untested ways of being and relating that nurture and support life instead of destroying it.

**

Ultimately, we have gathered together this multi-genre tome, in the understanding that truth and wisdom concerning pain, healing, and justice exist in multiple registers and forms. It is our sincere hope that one or some, if not all, of the pieces so generously and courageously shared by their authors meets you where you are at and nourishes and sustains your own resolve to heal, be a healer, and a justice worker. For if it is not already clear, let us leave no doubts, queridx reader: you, your family, your community, and the entire world we inhabit unquestionably deserve the peace and serenity that comes with healing and justice.

> *Sana sana colita de rana*
> *Si no sanas hoy*
> *Sanarás mañana*

May we heal today, tomorrow, and for generations to come.

PAIN
SPEAKING THAT WHICH WANTS TO REMAIN UNSPOKEN

Self-Care
Cynthia Estremera Gauthier

Self-immersed, blended, mixed with others
who take and consume, require so much of you.

Friends need your shoulders drenching you
with their tears and concerns. Children exhaust
your arms, breasts, and rest on your aching hips.

Your feet are tired of running after everyone
your back is breaking from labor.

Your eyes can barely see what's in front of you,
but you're expected to see what's all around you.

Your lover squeezes your heart and your
head is pounding from the way you hit
the pavement each rising morning of the sun.

Your goal; to be strong and unbreakable
Inside you're withering away professing
the need to be everywhere do everything,
morphing into a seven-armed goddess whose tears
never flow long enough to water her dried up gardens.

You continue to do and do and do until you can't do no more.

And they say "self-care."

Survival of self is more like it.

Self-care is for the privileged; those with time,
those with means and those with liberty.
Those who have the ability to breathe clean,
crisp air deep into their souls. Those who
don't have a care in the world . . .
not for those caring for their entire world.

Even when we are pushed to care for ourselves
it transforms into caring for others
evolving into self-sacrifice justified.

We never take the time to crack our hands,
backs, and hips. We justify our pain
as part of our life cycle.
Struggle is key to our self-survival,
but when will we thrive?

It's time to separate ourselves
Push away every grabbing, screaming,
pulling hand and voice gripping
and choking us.

If we don't put ourselves first,
how will we ever have the strength
to hold on, while everyone is dangling from our feet?

Counterstory as Catharsis: Alejandra's Deepest Wound

Aja Y. Martínez

Alejandra was seated on the couch, next to her abuela who was trembling a bit from the anxiety, and probably from the anticipation of grief. They sat on the precipice of a moment.

She reached out to reassuringly brush her abuela's silky soft hands—hands resting in her abuela's lap, fingers lightly intertwined as if in prayer.

Her abuela didn't look up, but slightly nodded, acknowledging Alejandra's gesture, and then both of their heads snapped up, startled at the voice that now spoke.

"He's asking to see you, Alé, he wants to speak with you." It was her uncle, her dad's eldest brother, Tio Tommy.

Alejandra looked across the room to where her mother was seated—and although Alejandra was 25 years old, already an adult and a mother herself to a young daughter, she sought the permission, or perhaps reassurance from her mother's slight nod to rise from her abuela's side and follow Tio Tommy to the bedroom and through the door that led to her Abuelo's deathbed.

Twenty Years Earlier

Alejandra was sitting, cuddled into her mother's abdomen—a perfectly carved out cubby for Alejandra's small five-year-old frame. Her baby brother lay adjacent to the couch, laughing and babbling in his bassinet, entertained for the moment by the cheerful children's tune playing on the TV as their mother's fingers dangled over the bassinet's edge, bobbing to the music's beat. Alejandra was slightly distracted by her brother's baby noises, as she focused intently on the lyrics of the song being sung by Winnie the Pooh and Piglet.

At the conclusion of the ditty Alejandra suddenly and matter-of-factly announced: "That happened to me!" Still smiling over at baby brother, slightly distracted, Alejandra's mother said, "Hm? What happened to you?"

"What Pooh and Piglet just said, Mami—someone I know touched my privates."

"What?" Mami responded, extracting her hand from my baby brother's grasp, abruptly sitting upright, nearly knocking Alejandra to the floor before catching her with both hands and righting her in a standing position on the ground.

Mami was seated, her back now rod-straight, staring searchingly into Alejandra's eyes, her own face etched with worry, searching Alejandra's face for any semblance of a smile, a joke, mere kidding or sarcasm of which she knew in her heart her five-year-old was incapable.

"Who touched your privates? You mean down there?" Mami questioned, pointing to Alejandra's pelvic area, a tone of panic seeping discernably into her voice. Alejandra, hesitating for a moment, noticed the tonal shift of her mother's voice, unsure if she had said something that upset her, unsure if she should say it again.

Perceptive to her daughter's uncertainty, Mami softened her tone and facial features—did her very best to come across as casual and conversational and asked again, "Who touched you, mija? Was it someone you know?" Alejandra solemnly nodded, then said, "It was Abuelo."

Twenty Minutes Later

A harsh set of knocks issued from the wrought iron screen door and Mami sprung from her seat on the couch. Barefoot, Mami hurriedly dashed to the door, unlocking the deadbolt to admit two tall male figures who Alejandra immediately recognized as Papi and his brother, Tio Tommy.

A smile spread across Alejandra's face, as she bounded from the couch to sprint towards her father, jumping into his arms.

Papi scooped her up, but held her at a slight distance, looking into her eyes. His eyes were somber and seemingly disconcerted. This look of anything but joy gave Alejandra pause now that she did the math adding her mother's perceptible tonal and energetic shift from before to her father's eyes and the looks of stern trepidation emanating from Tio Tommy.

Alejandra now inventoried the tense conversation she overheard only fifteen minutes before. Her mother, in frantic and hurried words, spoke to someone on the other end of the line, imparting a sense of urgency and eventual defensiveness, while Alejandra continued to view the Hundred Acre Wood Saturday Special that had now progressed to a song about "Stranger Danger."

"Why would I make this up?!" Mami exclaimed, sounding astounded, exasperated, and furious at the accusation, all at once. "This is the *last* thing I would *ever* say or do to get your attention—'to get you back'! How conceited are you? *Our* daughter has said a serious thing and we need to figure this out!"

That was the gist of what Alejandra was able to overhear of the conversation before her mother, seemingly successful in her persuasion, said "Okay, estamos aquí, see you soon," and hung up the phone.

And now, fifteen minutes later, Papi and Tio Tommy were here and told Alejandra they wanted to speak with her, alone in the kitchen, a room separated by a wall and a door from Mami, baby brother, and the TV. Alejandra looked across the room to where her mother was standing, for permission or perhaps reassurance? Her mother's slight nod made Alejandra nod her own head in acquiescence to her father and Tio Tommy's wishes.

After the Interrogation

Held tightly in Mami's arms, hoisted onto her hip, Alejandra waived goodbye to Papi and Tio Tommy as they drove away. Papi looked and sounded sad as he told Alejandra he'd be back in a couple of days to take her and baby brother to his place for dinner. Alejandra was happy to know she would see him again, having had a hard time adjusting to her parents' most recent separation which brought Papi around to take her and baby brother to his place only every other weekend. But before he left today with Tio Tommy, Papi asked Mami if he could see them more often, maybe a couple times a week, and Mami agreed. But they both looked so sad, and Alejandra couldn't figure out how the thought of seeing *more* of Papi could result in the melancholy she observed from her parents.

It didn't take long before Papi moved back in with Mami, Alejandra, and baby brother, but there was a noticeable shift in the ways Alejandra was permitted to interact with Papi's side of the family. For instance, whenever the cousins had birthday parties with sleepovers, Alejandra was never allowed to stay. She would beg, she would cry, she once even tried to thrash and rage, but all to no avail from Mami or Papi. There was some sort of armored and unbreakable pact now formed between the two of them—an understanding and renegotiation of the terms of their relationship, including what Alejandra understood as a prohibition against extended time and fun with los primos. And she didn't understand *why*.

As Alejandra grew older, into a teen, she became keenly aware of the gatherings she *wasn't* invited to, the bautismos in which she was *never* asked to be godmother, and the general bonds of familial relationships between and amongst the cousins and tios and tias on her dad's side of the family—all of which she felt excluded, blocked from, locked out of. And these observations caused Alejandra great pain. Mami, aware of her daughter's anguish, yet advisedly quiet about the root of this pain, decided it was time to reveal the true source of Alejandra's separation from her family. Knowing her daughter too well, Mami comprehended that Alejandra was taking these fissures personally. She invited Alejandra out for a drive and steadied herself for a conversation too long deferred.

The Roadtrip

"I knew there was something, but I couldn't ever put my finger on it," Alejandra responded, not shocked at the revelation, just surprised she hadn't pieced it together before now. Her body and her mind contained the memory of this abuse, this turmoil associated with the intrusion on her person, this assault of her very being. She remembered it *happening*. The room he took her to. The carefully selected cousins who were his victims alongside her. Her feelings of pleasure in the contact, feelings that now made her sick with revulsion and shame. She *remembered*.

"Why didn't you press charges?" Alejandra demanded, hot angry tears now welling in her eyes and rolling down her cheeks—revealing too much about her shame and anger—more than she wished to confirm.

"I did what I thought was best at the time, mija," answered Mami pleading discernably in her voice, which only made Alejandra angrier.

"He should be locked up!" Alejandra retorted, "How many has he done this to? How many has he hurt?!"

"I only found out about Tio Tommy's stepsons *after* what he did to you was revealed, I don't know how many else—"

"I do!" Alejandra interrupted. "I know cousin Jenny and Denise were there with me, I remember them on either side of me, I *remember!*"

Mami was crying now, which Alejandra had seen her do maybe twice in sixteen years. They drove on in silence for a moment, both crying silent tears, Alejandra's still searing with anger.

"I did what I thought was best at the time, mija," Mami repeated, more resolve in her voice now. "I thought that if we pressed charges, the legal system wouldn't protect you and I wanted to protect you from that. From being questioned by lawyers, dragged through a lawsuit. You were only five! I thought I was protecting you from further harm, I thought keeping you away from the possibility of it ever happening again and making clear to him that I *knew* what he did, and that he would *never* have access to you again was the way to handle it. I did what I thought was best—"

"And did that stop him from hurting others?" Alejandra demanded.

"I don't know" Mami responded, shaking her head, "I don't know."

As He Lay Dying

Alejandra followed Tio Tommy to the bedroom and through the door that led to her Abuelo's deathbed.

He looked grey in the weak light that seeped through the slats of the window blinds behind his hospital bed. He was laid out, a crumpled husk of a human, his breathing coming in shallow and staggered breaths.

Alejandra stood stock still in the doorway, uncertainty etched across her whole face and body, balanced on the balls of her feet, ready to swivel on a moment's notice, flight as her primary and most pressing bodily instinct. And then her Tia Blanca, seated in a far corner of the room near the head of Abuelo's bed said, "Come in Alé, it's okay. He's asked to see you."

Alejandra slowly walked to the side of the hospital bed and stood beside Tia Blanca—her dad's youngest sister. Tia Blanca and Alejandra stared into each other's eyes for an extended moment and Alejandra was transported into a memory of the previous day, when she heard Tia Blanca's raised voice yelling through tears in an adjacent room.

Alejandra had been sitting in the den, in silent vigil once again, just like today, at her abuela's side—sometimes holding Abuela's hand, sometimes resting her head on Abuela's shoulder while Abuela lightly stroked Alejandra's hair. And she heard in the adjacent living room what sounded like a lively arrangement of family conversation—not uncommon for this large and boisterous Mexican familia—erupting into fury.

"Why didn't anyone protect us?!" Tia Blanca exclaimed. "I'm the last of *twelve* kids! Why didn't this stop the first time he did this? Why didn't anyone protect us?!" At this outcry there was further eruption of weeping from many more of Alejandra's tias—six sisters in total to match the six brothers of which her dad was one. A family of twelve children. Twenty-four years or so of Alejandra's abuela being constantly and consistently pregnant. So many years *he* had access to her abuela's body. And Abuela, in her youth, was this family's first victim.

Simona's Story

When Abuela was diagnosed with stage IV breast cancer—ten years after Abuelo's death—Alejandra made a point of sitting with Abuela Simona to collect and record her stories, every Sunday, for the nearly three months she had left on this earth.

Abuela's stories ranged from tales of her childhood in the nearby bordertown, her own mother's death at too young an age, her father's quick re-marriage to a woman who thought Simona and her siblings a burden, and her close relationship with her own abuela who ended up raising her when her new stepmother made it clear Simona and her siblings were not welcome in her father's new familial configuration. Some of Abuela Simona's stories were funny, many were sad, but the story of how she became Abuelo's wife was infuriating, and revelatory.

As Simona told it, she met Abuelo when she was still in high school—when she was a seventeen-year-old junior, who loved school, was brilliant at math, and had ambitions to one day become a bookkeeper. Quite the dreams for a 1940s-era Mexican woman. Then, Abuelo, a man ten years her senior, began vying for her attention and eventually caught her eye. She insisted she was a dedicated "school-girl," a "good-girl" who was "raised right" and wanted to make her abuela and her father proud. She was somewhat flattered and enthralled by the attention Abuelo cast her way—he was edgy and seemed exciting—James Dean before James Dean was a thing. And she was a child. Young, naïve, idealistic, and not at all prepared to be in the clutches of a sexual predator.

Their dates started out innocent enough. He would meet her after school, they would grab a bite to eat and ride around in his car until nearly dusk, when Simona insisted on being taken home and dropped off two blocks from her abuela's house so she could feign walking home from the after-hours tutoring she told her abuela she was attending. She felt guilty lying about her whereabouts in this way, especially to her beloved abuela—but this romance was thrilling, and from Simona's inexperienced perspective, innocent.

It wasn't until nearly a month into their weekly dates he told her he had a surprise for her—he had plans to take her somewhere they'd never gone before. And turns out, that place was nearly 300 miles from her hometown—so far away that there was no way she could return to her home before sunset that day, let alone sunrise the next day—so far away that in that time, in that era, there was no way to return home anything other than a ruined woman.

Alejandra didn't have the nerve or the heart to ask Abuela Simona if he had raped her that night. All Abuela Simona offered, as the conclusion to that story was that she had no choice but to marry him after the stunt he pulled. There was no other option, and thus commenced Simona's journey with this man.

When Abuela Simona was on her own death bed, not long after she revealed this story to Alejandra, she made clear to her daughters that under no circumstances did she wish to be buried with him. She made clear that she had lain with him enough in this life and she had no desire to be laid to rest with him as well. She had her reasons.

Reflecting on her Abuela Simona's life with this predator, this abuser, the sexual criminal who abused all of Simona's children, and many of her grandchildren, Alejandra reckons with the realization that Abuela Simona was the family's first victim.

The Shame Beats So Long as His Heart

Alejandra reached her hand out to hold Tia Blanca's and then broke the gaze they had been sustaining. She redirected her gaze to stare down at the shrunken figure of Abuelo and stated clearly and loudly: "Estoy aquí." His eyelids slowly opened, seemingly too great a burden to bear for extended periods of time. He looked up and into Alejandra's hovering eyes and his eyes filled with tears. He made a feeble gesture with one of his gnarled and claw-like hands and Alejandra felt Tia Blanca's hand squeeze her own.

Abuelo mouthed a few words, perhaps a phrase—too raspy and indiscernible for Alejandra to comprehend, and Alejandra narrowed her eyes, doing her best to understand. Tio Tommy, misunderstanding Alejandra's narrowed eyes as ire jumped up from his seat on the opposite side of the bed from Tia Blanca and said, "He's asking for your forgiveness. He wants you to let him go in peace."

Alejandra looked from Tio Tommy back down to Abuelo for confirmation of this request, and Abuelo slowly and seemingly painfully nodded his head in concurrence. Many thoughts rushed into Alejandra's mind as her brain, her body, her very being began shouting inside her head all at once:

"Why now?! He's had TWENTY years to make amends, why now?! You're a mother now to little Sofi! Could you EVER forgive someone who did this to HER?! He HURT you! He hurt so many— and he wants PEACE?! What about the rest of us who have to live with the trauma and terror he's inflicted?! He gets to leave in peace?! He gets to put the burden of peace on his victims?! FUCK HIM!"

Alejandra's mind was racing, and she felt the expectant gaze of Tio Tommy on her as well as the nervous anticipation communicated through Tia Blanca's hand. And all of a sudden Alejandra was a five-year-old little girl again who just wanted her mommy. Tears began streaming from her lowered eyes and she shook her head and muttered over and over, "I want my mom, please go get Mami, I want my mommy, get my mom—"

Motivated and seemingly horrified by Alejandra's devolvement from a woman in her mid-twenties to a crying child, Tio Tommy darted from the room and hurriedly returned with Mami who flew to her crying child's side, placing a protective arm around Alejandra's shoulders.

As if sensing Mami's presence, Abuelo's eyes snapped open. He then raised his head slightly, fully alert and focusing on Mami. "Quiero que me perdones" Abuelo rasped—never qualifying *what* he wanted forgiveness for, even though everyone in the room *knew* for what offense he was begging Mami's forgiveness.

Mami, looking him straight in the eyes responded, "No es para mi a perdonar," she said, shaking her head and pointing a finger to her chest. "Solo Dios" she continued, pointing her finger to the sky, "perdonar," she finished, pointing the same finger to him. She said this without cruelty or malice; it was just an expression of her beliefs.

Abuelo slowly closed his eyes, nodded his head, and lowered it once more to the pillow.

***

Mami and Alejandra left the bedroom, resuming their respective places within the house—waiting, waiting, waiting, as relatives cycled their way in and out of the space, saying their farewells.

Seated again beside Abuela, Alejandra held her hand, cycling together through rosary beads. Then, midway through their third decade of the rosary sequence, Papi—Alejandra's father and Abuela's son—emerged from Abuelo's bedroom and said, "It's time."

Alejandra rose and extended her hand to Abuela, who shook her head "no" and did not stand. "I'll stay with her" said Mami, rising from her chair across the room, taking Alejandra's place beside Abuela.

Following Papi, Alejandra re-entered Abuelo's bedroom, taking her place around his bed among her cousins, aunts, and uncles. As Abuelo inhaled and exhaled his final breaths, Alejandra's eyes surveyed the room looking from face to face of abuse victim after abuse victim. She reflected on the intense homophobia she had experienced from the males in this family—wondering about a connection to their abuse. She was struck by the intense fear and vulnerability she knew her female aunts and cousins projected as they navigated their worlds in relation to men. And what was most astounding of all to Alejandra in this moment, was that she knew in her heart nearly everyone gathered around that bed, victims that they were, had a true sense of love and devotion to this man.

Alejandra's ears called her focus back from her musings, back from the victims' faces, back to the face of the abuser they had in common as he breathed in and then out for the final time. Minutes later, breaking the family's silence and tears, a cousin pointed out that Abuelo's chest seemed to continue beating with a heartbeat's pulse. An aunt responded, "It's his pacemaker. It's a mechanical heart—it looks like his heart is beating, but it's not real."

Counterstory is
catharsis
Counterstory is
this storyteller's praxis for
radical
healing and
justice.
Counterstory as
methodology
provides this author an outlet
by which to surface buried personal
and family shame,
to pour it out of her body like venom
or possibly antibody
for another.
Counterstory is vision—
it is seeing, re-seeing, differently seeing, truly seeing
this story.
Counterstory
brings healing.
brings justice.
radical healing and justice.
Let. Me. See.
Sana, Sana, Colita de Rana. . .

The Collective Body

Susana Victoria Parras

I want to experience collective healing
how I experience crying:
Free. Complex. Layered. Unapologetic.

I want to heal how I cry in safety:
Dignified. Free of shame.
The collective body and spirit are mangled.
I see how deeply the collective body hurts.
How deeply it wants to punish and destroy.
Taken hostage long ago by the seductions
of dominance and power.

We are unrecognizable to each other.
We fear what we don't know.

We want to destroy and punish what we don't know.
We don't know each other.

We are unrecognizable to each other.
We destroy and are destroyed.
We don't have to continue like this. This is not ours.
The unnecessary eons of suffering and death,
endless pain, it's not ours. We did not create oppression,
but we learned how to reproduce it.

I am committed to nurturing relationships as vehicles
of transforming pain housed in our bodies and relationships.

Death structures and logics that disconnect, dehumanize
and disembody us need to be destroyed.
No more destruction onto the collective body.
No more destruction onto the individual body.
We move towards building relationships where bodies
are free and safe to express their endless spectrums
of love, rage, and grief.

Perpetual Chillona

Daisy Muñoz

Edgar Fabian Frias: *"¿Qué te hubiera gustado escuchar de niñx?"*

Memory dwells on the insults,
linguistically manipulated
verbalized terror, defining
my worth in a dehumanizing manner.
Branded into my childhood subconscious
is a tailored dictionary of labels:

Puerca, Marrana, Sucia,
Inservible, Inútil, Estúpida,
Hija de tu Chingada Madre,
Gorda, Fea, Babosa.
How was I to defend myself
from the sharp words stabbing
into my childhood psyche?
It's strange how the auditory enters
and never leaves from its crevices.
Memories held against my will,
my ear canals are open to all
and I receive more than I want.

"Mírate en el espejo,"
my mother grabbed me by the shoulders—
"Mira que fea te ves,"
forced onto my own reflection.
I was met with a sobbing girl,
bloodshot, swollen eyes,
snot dripping down, tears
traced onto the curves
of my full cheeks.
She was I and I was she.
"Grábatelo," my mom seethed
through her clenching jaw.
Hay palabras que nunca se olvidan.

How do you remove trauma
branded upon your memory?
The worst insults were always delivered
by my parents in their mother tongue.
Show me, how do I give a funeral
to words that inflict pain?
I'll gladly pay for the coffins and the service.

Writing the Storm

Daniel Shank Cruz

"the deit[y] of creative destruction"[1]—*Guabancex, the Taíno Goddess of Storms*

I'm thinking about silence. I'm thinking about the racism I internalized as a half-Nuyorican, half-white boy growing up in the Bronx. I'm thinking about how my all-white Mennonite church erased my Latinidad and taught me to erase my sexuality; how the church taught me discipline instead of love; how my white mother and Puerto Rican father let that happen; how they didn't teach me Spanish; how knowing one colonizer's language might be too much anyway; how I didn't hear the word "Taíno" until I was in my thirties because colonialism still bleeds; how I'm ready to stop being silent and look to Guabancex to help me tear the doors off and learn to build something from the rubble.

When my abuela molested me, I was ten years old, sitting on my bed while watching the television she had given me for Christmas the year before. She and my grandpa, Pop, were making a rare visit to my house. Even though they only lived a fifteen-minute drive across the Bronx, my parents, sister, and I almost always visited them so that we could enjoy my abuela's cooking and so that we could also visit my uncle, who lived in the upstairs apartment. I don't remember why she and Pop were visiting that night. The adults were talking in the living room, and I got bored, so I went to my room. The TV was a small black-and-white with a screen that couldn't have been more than nine inches across. Even as a kid, when she gave it to me, my first reaction was "they still make black-and-white TVs?" It was 1989, and the only other black-and-white I had ever encountered was

---

1 Aurora Levins Morales, *Kindling: Writing on the Body* (Cambridge, MA: Palabrera Press, 2013), 5.

at my other grandparents' house. They upgraded to a color set when I was three or four.

Enveloped in its scent of Lysol mixed with the frying oil from chicharrones, my abuela's house was a party. I could have all the Pepsi and potato chips I wanted. Once when I was there, she let me eat so many dill pickles that I threw up all over the kitchen floor, the dark green pickle flecks a semi-digested constellation in a puddle of yellow liquid. She let me watch as much TV as I desired during the day, though Saturday nights were reserved for her to watch *Sábado Gigante*. I would watch along with her and Pop so that I could see Univision's sign-off with a cartoon beagle brushing his teeth and singing "hasta mañana" at the end of the night. He looked like Underdog, but with a sky-blue sleeping cap and gown instead of a cape. My life at her house was very different than my life at home, where snacks and TV time were both strictly limited. Although she was probably aware of this snack regulating, I don't know whether she knew that I was only allowed to watch a half hour of non-PBS programming a week unless my father was watching sports on the weekend. I'm sure she thought having my own TV would delight me. As it was, its smallness and lack of color meant that I hardly used it.

That night I was bored, so I went to my room and looked for something to watch. The living room at the front of the house was far enough away from my room that I could keep my door open without disturbing anyone or being disturbed by the others. After about fifteen minutes, my abuela came in and sat next to me. She started rubbing my back, which felt like a normal show of affection. Then her hand went under the band of my sweatpants and underwear and began exploring. I had not hit puberty yet, but I remember an overwhelming tingly feeling washing over me as we sat there; a feeling that I now recognize as arousal. After maybe ten minutes, she got up and left, and I stayed sitting there. Soon afterwards, she and Pop went home.

Aside from monthly daytime Saturday visits to their house with my father, my younger sister and I would sleep over on weekends once in a while so my parents could have some time alone together. The way Pop and my abuela spoiled us made my overactive imagination suspicious because of how decadent it was. This decadence was especially extended to me as a male. My abuela would make my sister help her grate plantains for pasteles around the holidays while I got to stay on the couch in front of the TV. When we accompanied her on the bus to the TSS department store, she would always buy me a G.I. Joe, but only sometimes buy my sister something. I knew this was unfair but didn't protest. Abuela was an adult, she could do what she wanted. Church taught me to submit to authority, so I just enjoyed my toys.

I sensed a difference between my abuela and Pop and my sister and me that was something other than our age. They were working with a sensual knowledge that was absent from our house. The radio was louder, food was more savory, bodies were more on display. I fantasized about them being some kind of spies, building our trust for some malevolent purpose like the witches in fairytales who fattened children up for eating later. Then I would laugh at myself for how silly this sounded.

Abuela would have me sleep in her bed with her when we visited and have my sister sleep on the pull-out couch because she said my sister flailed around too much in her sleep for the two of them to be in the same bed. Pop would sleep on a rollaway bed in the dining room. My sister and I didn't question this arrangement despite my sister's jealousy about me sleeping with Abuela. She was our favorite grandparent because of how much she spoiled us (our other grandparents lived in Virginia, so they didn't get the opportunity to spoil us as much because we only got to see them once or twice a year), so we both wanted to be in her bed. But now that I think about these sleeping arrangements, they make no sense. Why were Pop and Abuela not sleeping in the same bed, with me and my sister on the couch, or one of us on the couch and one on the rollaway bed? What was going on when I was asleep?

I have never told anyone in my family about the night in my bedroom. I did not tell anyone until I was in college, when I told my faculty advisor and a few close friends. I've mostly tried to ignore what happened. Its existence muddles the happy memories I have of my abuela that I wish I could focus on instead. I've had a mostly fortunate life, so it's tempting to just pretend the incident never happened and to censor it, pulling it out of the tapestry of my life's story. I want to ignore the word "incest." But doing so would be another act of violence.

I was molested. It's a common experience, unfortunately. What is the point of putting it in print, of sharing it with strangers? I try to understand my molestation within the context of other societal ills. Ultimately my abuela was responsible for her actions and blame lies with her, but other social mores helped create a setting where such an event could occur. In earlier years,

Pop cheated on her with impunity because that's what machismo taught Latinx men of his generation to do. Maybe she was trying to exercise some power over me as a way of counteracting the powerlessness he must have made her feel. Her reversing of the stereotypical roles of abuse as a woman abusing a boy, which works to make the act illegible because of the societal assumption that molesters are always men, was one facet of this power.

My lack of sex education at the time also played a role. This deprivation was partly a mark of our body-hating culture and partly a result of my family's Mennonite beliefs that made sexual discourse unspeakable. I didn't say anything when it happened because my abuela was an adult, and she was a family member, two statuses that made her someone I was supposed to trust and obey. She would often bathe me when I was younger, and sometimes take baths with me and my sister. In some ways what happened on my bed seemed like the same kind of touching as drying me off. It was unclear where the lines of what was acceptable and what was not were. It is not my fault that I did not have this knowledge, and the failure to convey it to me made me powerless to resist that night or to even recognize that I had been violated so my parents could keep me safe in the future. Several years after Abuela molested me, Pop molested my sister. If I had been taught enough to speak up about my own abuse, maybe she could have been saved from that violence. This same lack of language made it impossible for me to realize I was queer until I left the church in college. It's a lack intertwined with the silencing of my boricua history, which remains marginal, confined largely to books by small independent publishers. I haunt libraries and bookstores looking for it, working to construct a healed decolonized self.

My abuela is in her late eighties now, living out her last years with dementia. A confrontation with her about the incident in which I sought some sort of apology or reconciliation would be futile; I am willing to let it lie. Writing about it instead is my revenge. A poster of Guabancex hangs above my thriftstore desk. I watch her move and write myself into being.

You're Not a Regular Mexican

Jennifer Hernandez Lankford

I knew exactly what it meant to be white from my peers at a proud Blue Ribbon School in an affluent neighborhood of Dallas, Texas. It meant being important, being appreciated, being beautiful, having a voice. I knew being Brown meant I was out not in, different, weird, and other. This left me no room to embrace what made me so special. What I didn't know was how to authentically love myself and that the melanin in my skin embodied a long line of strength, resilience, and beauty.

My second-generation mother of a Mexican immigrant made my education a top priority. This meant living in tiny efficiencies or using a false address to keep me from going to a second-rate school. Education was her ticket to make ourselves seen and to shatter the ceilings we looked up at from day one. Like so many before her, she was fighting to ensure a future for herself and her child. She was only doing what she knew to be the best she could. Years of instilling this idea that my academic ability defined my significance meant I made it my business to be a top student. I stayed on the honor roll, was recruited for the talented and gifted program and was asked to take the SAT for a pilot program run by Duke University in the sixth grade. I'm almost certain this was why I was allowed to stay enrolled at this particular school. We carefully tiptoed around district lines trying not to let on that we didn't always live within the boundary. Although, I find it hard to believe they didn't have an inkling we weren't always living within district lines. I watched other Brown kids quickly get ousted for living outside the district, including a family member. However, these were kids that didn't excel academically and had too many special needs. I, on the other hand, helped them shine a light on how "they" could help children "like me," an at-risk student, defined as eligible for the National School Lunch Program (which I was always on to get a warm meal), succeed, despite my poor socio-demographic status. A token story that "closing the gap" was on "their" agenda and "look how well it is going!"

Still, I was comparing myself to people who had no concept of what it meant to be other. Deep down, I wanted to have thin hair that fit perfectly into French braids. Instead, I had thick hair with a wave I didn't know how to tame. I wanted to be skinny and wear skinny girl preppy clothes. Instead, I had a little panza from too many mornings of eating the tortilla masa my grandma used to make. So, I mostly wore looser shirts covered by zip up sweaters for an extra layer of hiding. Hiding wasn't a luxury afforded to me. No matter how badly I wanted to escape my brown skin, my wavy hair or belly there was nowhere to hide. My last name, Hernández, always gave me away. I wore it like a badge of shame. The first time I really felt embarrassed by it was after one of those skinny, preppy, white peers of mine looked at me with disgust and said, "There's Jenny Hernan*DEZ*," emphasizing the DEZ part with extra malice. Why she hated my name, I didn't know, but I knew the feeling it gave me. It reinforced that I didn't belong.

I thought there was an understanding between me and other kids with different shades of skin. We naturally gravitated toward each other for reasons we didn't know how to articulate. It just was. It was as if this circle we drew around ourselves encapsulated our safety. If one of us fell out of the ring, then we'd extend a hand pulling us back to our secure cocoon of a community. We played on each other's dodge ball teams in PE, sat together at lunch, and chopped it up on the playground.

One very important thing we had in common was the shape of our bodies. We were curvier, rounder, and showing womanhood long before our white counterparts. Everyone else noticed it too. In the fifth grade, one of my good friends, let's call her Krystal, started her period. It was all anyone could talk about. That red stain that led her home for two days left us murmuring about what it meant for our group. Now, one of our own had transformed into this extraordinary being of wonder. We were so engulfed by this change to her body as if it had happened to all of us.

Krystal's womanhood was now something we all had to bear. Fear crept into my bloodstream and the uncertainty grew into a ball of anxiety in the pit of my stomach. Not only was she dark skinned, but now she added yet another mark of difference we didn't know how to answer for. When she came back to school, we gathered around her with all the usual questions. Did it hurt? What did her boyfriend say? When would it happen to us? Did she feel changed?

"You don't need to worry," Krystal told me un-phased, "my mom said it probably won't happen to the white girls as soon." I was shook. White girl? Was she talking about me? All this time I thought we had an understanding that we shared the same color skin, sisterhood, friendship even, and here she was calling me a white girl!

"I'm not white . . . " I said in a quiet voice.

"Well, you're not Black!" she said loudly and matter of fact. This sent me reeling into a panic of questions. I knew I wasn't white. My skin wasn't white, my name wasn't white, and my family at home did not look like the white families I saw on TV. So who, *what* was I? It wasn't a conversation I had with my mom or anyone in my family. I held it in because facing these questions was uncomfortable and frankly, embarrassing. The ambiguity of my being settled into a comfortable silence I found solace in. I finally found my hiding place in the corner called shame. Deep seeded, grown, and rooted shame cared for by everyone around me. I wasn't white, I wasn't Black. I was unsure of where I belonged. I felt unpretty, unworthy, and unsure of myself.

Years passed until my adolescence brought on an even bigger identity struggle. I was a book nerd who liked Harry Potter, wanted to prove I was not like everyone else, but still cared about what everyone thought deep down. I was incredibly awkward, so naturally I chose to wear clothes from Hot Topic, listen to punk music, and wear black eyeliner. I guess you could call me your typical teenager. The one part of me I could not give up on was my incessant need to prove myself academically. By this time, my mother moved us to the cheapest apartment she could find in a more affluent suburb of the city to ensure the quality of my education. I was in competition with mostly rich, white kids and Asian immigrants to stay at the top of my class.

The first week of tenth grade biology I was paired with a kid from China as my lab partner. He had just moved to the US but told me immediately he thought biology would be an easy class despite his limited English. He shared that anything less than an A would get him into trouble with his father. I didn't think much of it at the time, but he was sizing me up. Was I, a Brown girl, going to help or hurt his efforts to achieve his A in this science class? Judging from the way he looked at me with contempt that first week and ignored me most days during lecture he didn't expect much from me. I was fine with that because being invisible was my specialty—my preference even.

Then, our first exam came. I studied hard, knew most of the answers and finished 30 minutes before the bell rang with time to put my head down for a nap. He shook his head as I turned in my test. I assume he thought I blew it off and just didn't care about my score. So, the next week when we received our test back and I had a big red 92% on the front his eyes filled with surprise. An A I had worked for, an A I earned, an A I expected out of myself even though no one else did. He gawked at my paper. When he saw the red 85% on his test his eyes filled with shock and horror. Finally, the words I will never forget escaped his mouth, "You're not a *regular* Mexican!"

Those words embodied the sentiment I had carried on my conscience for so long. That Mexicans, like my grandma, my mom, and myself had one expectation on us from society. The expectation that we have no intelligence to succeed in any way that mattered and failed to prove otherwise. In retrospect, I realize he didn't see me. He saw the color of my skin; he saw what he was told to expect from people that look like me. When I looked at myself, I saw someone who never had anyone to advocate for her body, her being, her identity. That idea that I wasn't white, I wasn't Black or even a "regular Mexican" weighed heavily on my ability to have self-love—blocked it even.

For years, I thought of all the Brown girls, women and people who deal with feeling unpretty in their skin. For years, my heart ached that I, along with them, felt no agency or pride in how remarkable we truly are. For years, my eyes stung with tears of disgrace for my people and myself.

I've never felt normal. Not quite here nor there, never meeting all expectations of normalcy, but checking just enough boxes to not draw attention. I grew up being used to unnervingly walking a tightrope between visible and invisible. The ambiguity of my identity began to not only take hold of me, carefully defining my self-worth. It was as if holding myself in a space of non-being became a safety net, a way to survive and a way to avoid answering any tough questions about my existence. I didn't need anyone to dehumanize me because society had convinced me I could do that myself. I wasn't human enough to be seen, but just human enough to take up valuable space. It was this design that made me feel like a burden to others. I should count myself lucky for any ounce of opportunity, worth and love I could muster. Writing itself into my DNA, this sentiment wrapped itself around my heart, leading to years of low self-esteem and feelings of unworthiness. At least this was the narrative reeling through my malleable brain in elementary school. My caramel skin, a beautiful mix of every shade handed down by my ancestors, left people perplexed. More importantly, it left me in a state of identity limbo.

Until now.

I spent years before my children's birth seeking out therapies for my diagnosed depression and anxiety. I was met with a string of counselors who often cited my pain and feelings of unworthiness as something I can simply "change with cognitive behavioral therapy." They handed me pages of "how to change your thoughts" type resources, pointing the finger right back at me. The problem with this is it doesn't address the social system we live in that perpetuates racial oppression and encourages my feelings of self-loathing. I left these sessions feeling exhausted and broken. I felt it was my duty to "fix" my messed-up brain and it was hard work that I had to do on my own. I felt alone and at the mercy of my very own chemical make up. Then I heard about culturally competent therapy—the concept that therapy could and should reflect a person's background and culture. I needed a therapist who understood me as a Latinx woman with many different levels of complex racial and ethnic experiences that intersected with my depression and anxiety. My new therapist (a Latina and mother) truly saw me, empathized with my experience, and had the skills to help me heal that inner little Brown girl searching for self-love. Finally, I formed a therapeutic relationship with someone who understood me more than any of her prior white counterparts. My healing had begun in my sessions with her diving into deep-rooted pains from my past. We did several sessions of EMDR (eye movement desensitization and reprocessing) where I sobbed and felt the pain engulf my entire body some days. I left her office each time feeling like the weight of the world had been lifted from my spirit. What I accomplished in those sessions outweighed the years of therapy I had done before. I felt empowered to conquer the trauma living inside my body and I had real agency over it for the first time ever.

My concept of self began to change especially after I gave birth to two beautiful babies of my own. I had to reckon with my shame. I used the power of my body, breath, and voice to bring both of my babies into this world and never felt more powerful than I did in those moments. I distinctly remember my doula whispering into my ear "you were meant for this," and feeling like nothing had been truer. I had spent so much of my life trying to prove my significance in this world by earning degrees, awards, and accolades and left empty in the process. But in giving life to these humans, I learned my strength physically, emotionally, mentally, and beyond. I suddenly felt like a warrior ready for battle. Where my shame lived comfortably in my soul before, was now replaced with irrevocable pride and pure love. How, I asked myself, could I ever feel ashamed of these beings. It was now up to me to help them realize the story in their melanin is one of resilience and insurmountable worthiness. The fact that their value as humans would and will undoubtedly be questioned because of their skin color helped me access a fiery healing energy to be proud and full of love not only for my babies, but also for myself.

I wasn't born where the earthquakes are hitting

Frankie A. Soto

I am more than my clumsy tongue falling over itself/ fumbling
palabras I could never seem to grip tight enough to ease my
Abuelas ears from bleeding with sharp miscues of words/ I double dutched two languages always getting my foot caught on the
rope/ my mouth wanted to be a homeland without an asterisk/
I am many asterisks after my last name they will ask but do you
speak spanish?/ I will shrug a mixture of no in sign language and
silence/ my tongue has always been a bystander watching con-
versations/watching the rope twirl waiting for my turn to jump
in/ waiting to stop reasoning that my sangre isn't a trespasser/
even if my mouth is a rebel who has yet to speak the way of my
ancestors/ I want my pain to not need an explanation /I want
my worry to be my accent to be my mourning of land that my
Wela rose from/the cracks there are so many cracks in the earth/
it is shaking the life out of the breathing/ They haven't caught
their wind after Maria/are they alive?/ is this what aftershock
feels like/ a president with an empty wallet/ mentirosa/ lies and
wigs/ carnivorous ground with an endless appetite/ Trump with
an endless twitter/ a mother uses her body as armor from the
crumbled ceiling/ her daughter still doesn't make it/ she does/ a
purge will begin soon/ the land is evicting its tenants/ asking for
rent/ asking for overdue help/ never asking if I speak spanish/
Just asking to be heard/ to not be forgotten in playas/ in resorts/
in San Juan on a brisk evening of white on white slacks and un-
buttoned shirts/ falling over on the way home/ drunk on a heavy
handed bartenders pour/ rum in your step/ the sugar keeping
you moving/ a clumsy salsa en route to finding a hotel key card/
a heartbeat that is rumbling/ you don't look at the ground/ you
don't look at the people who don't have a return flight some-
where/ a home that isn't dying/ a casket burying itself.

How to tell my Novio, Mamá, Abuela

Lysz Flo

I get defensive at the word *black* spilling
from a mouth that forgets our roots

that for me to be in this skin is to be unequipped
for wars I never knew I signed up for.

To exist as mujer, negra, natural, is to defend
the dissertation of things people doubt me being

To teach Mi Novio, that calling them crows
is to remind me, that we are not an us.

Separating them and us is my reminder
of the daily fragmentation of who I really am

Ser una negra fina spills from the lips
of my grandmother, as if fitting outside a mold

makes me question; if I wasn't your granddaughter
would I still be *pretty for a Black girl*?

Mama, it's complicated, I am so angry
if only you could understand:

I carry the rage of the Haitian revolution in my skin
I carry the curse of its inability to rise above the
corruption of its roots, in my veins
I carry the abandonment of the colonizer
in my heartbeat with each rejection
in my Boricua existence.

Despite our type of Black we'd be persecuted the same,
this defiance isn't just in me, it's the ancestors telling me

they should know better

But how do I tell my Novio, Mama, and Wela
about their undying colonialism?

Grieving in Spanglish: A Glossary of Loss

Christian A. Bracho

> <u>Dolor: (n).</u> A state of great sorrow or distress; pain. Middle English (denoting both physical and mental pain or distress): via Old French from Latin dolor 'pain, grief'.[1]

The first time I really encountered dolor was when my mom lost her grandmother, my Mama Leonor. I remember my mother's heaving sobs in the hallway the day Mama Leonor died, and I recall my cousin Rocio throwing up in the car the day of the funeral. I remember my Tio Pepe and Tia Cata shaking at the gravesite, and the many times I found my Mom crying in her room in the weeks and months that followed. Then came years of weekly visits to the panteón with the family, visiting Mama Leonor every Sunday to pray, sing sad Catholic laments in Spanish, like "altisimo señor," and my brother and I would wander around the green lawns to read old gravestones from the 1940s and 50s. Our weekly visits went on for at least six or seven years, making our way from the deep San Gabriel Valley town of La Puente to the green hills of Glendale. In those years, I received a veritable education in grief—not that wishy-washy American grief, that white grief, that gringo grief, that "you have to go through the stages of grief!" grief. No.

---

1 Each entry in this glossary—my compendium of *dolor*—represents a journey through dictionaries, etymologies, and mitología, transcending languages and signs to discern a Spanglish gem beneath. I surfaced these definitions through digital and print explorations of: *The American Heritage Dictionary*, especially its Indo-European root appendix; the *Diccionario Etimologico Castellano En Linea*, curated by Valentín Anders and multiple collaborators (http://etimologias. dechile.net/); *Merriam-Webster Dictionary*, which offered insights into cognates and cousins of words; the canonical *Real Academia Española*, which clarified contemporary meanings and historical referents; and the wildly creative *Online Etymology Dictionary* (https://www.etymonline.com/), a work that is in itself the labor of another curious bard traveling through words and worlds, looking for those hidden gems.

I think Mexican grief is something else. Dolor, or duelo, is a committed, loving, grueling encounter with death and loss. It is a doting love, quantified and qualified by tears, gritos, silent curses, candles lit, altars built, rosaries prayed. It is the encounter with the other world as a regular and even ordinary aspect of life, going about your everyday in a relationship with loss. That is how my mom grieved her mom, and then my dad, when his cancer got the best of him. Watching her, I learned the meaning of dolor. What it means to honor our dead.

Grief in the US instead feels like a process of moving from one stage to the next, ending with reconciliation, some magical moment when the sufferer of grief raises a fist to the sky and says "Finally, I'm ready to live again!" Gringo grief is a process to be completed; a neat integration and moving on from loss. Even that famous cycle of grief by Elisabeth Kübler-Ross—denial, anger, bargaining, depression, acceptance—was articulated based on her research with people who were going to die, *not* the people who were left behind. Naturally, for the folks who must confront their mortality, acceptance is an important and final step.

But my grief is not like that. My dolor, the pain of losing mis papás, means encountering anguish daily, with arms open. My people don't turn away from it; we make space for it, create language and ritual for it. Dolor is the viuda who cries for her husband even 20 years after he is gone; it is the hija's dutiful visit to the graveyard every Sunday to pray a rosary, wipe the headstone clean, and leave fresh flowers. Duelo is that thing that makes this devoted son listen to *Amor Eterno*—both the Rocio Durcal and Juan Gabriel versions, thank you very much—on repeat, and letting the tears flow as I sing *como quisieraaaaa que tuuuuu vivierasss*. It is finally finding the traditional marigolds, the cempasúchil, at the random florist in Pomona that you spent an hour trying to find. It is crying as you make your Día de Muertos altar at the end of October, when the holy season truly begins. It is not something that "finishes." There is no magical moment. No end.

Maybe because I grieve in Spanglish, I do not imagine—or want—an end to dolor. My mother, my father, all my people, they do not deserve to be relegated to memory. My dolor is present and active; it animates their spirits.

My dolor is what keeps them alive.

Herencia: (n.) something that is passed down from preceding generations; a tradition. From Old French, *heredite*, inheritance, from Latin *hērēd-*, heir. From Indo-European *ghe-*: to release, let go.

When I was little, the dictionary was one of my best friends. I remember hours and hours spent flipping through the pages of that thick, red *American Heritage Dictionary*, discovering new words, reading sample sentences, and wondering how words came to be what they meant. In the back of that dictionary was a glossary of Indo-European roots, which, at eleven and twelve years old, I remember imagining as the great, great, great grandparents of words we use today. Some of the definitions in the dictionary directed the reader to the root, which revealed the DNA of the word, its origins in ancient utterances that evolved through time and space. Flipping from the dictionary to the glossary, I was a scavenger going backward in time, from written word to oral tradition, discovering a magical gem inside each etymological womb.

Growing up, English words came easily to me at school, but at home, I struggled to keep up with the Spanish my parents spoke, that my older siblings used with them, or that my cousins rapid-fire uttered when they visited at Christmas. Speaking Spanish felt like having peanut butter in my mouth—like I knew what I wanted to say, and maybe even the words in my head to say them, but my mouth was too gooey. Maybe it was because my parents worked so hard—my dad as a waiter at Acapulco in Atwater Village, my mom doing overtime at the factory or juggling a side job at KMart. Catching them on the weekends, I became more fluent in Spanglish, living full pocho, between two tongues, two heritages, two wombs.

One of my favorite things to do with my mom was watching Mexican telenovelas. The first I remember was *Rosa Salvaje*, that one with a 35-year-old Veronica Castro acting like a teenage tomboy who stumbles into the wealthy Casa Linares and ends up marrying one of the twin brothers. Years later, we were hooked on *La Madrastra*, and would sit in her room and watch each capítulo in semi-silence, gasping at something shocking or laughing at something stupid. When I moved far away for school, we talked on the phone or FaceTimed daily, checking in to make sure we were both okay. It wasn't until after she died that I realized those novela giggles and calls were my daily doses of Spanish. Losing her meant losing touch with that daily tongue, those palabras, that melody you only hear in español.

A few months after she died, I was desperate to hear and live in Spanish again, so I took a Spanish class. I reasoned it was to stay fluent, but I realized midway through the semester I was trying to hold on to my parents, who I wrote about in my homework. I even wrote a short story in Spanish about a sad boy living in a snowy city coming out to his mama over the phone—an admittedly more biographical than fictional tale! All around me people were telling me in English to remember good times, that time heals all wounds, that my mother was at peace. In that class, as I spoke, wrote, and conjugated Spanish, I was able to fully live in my *dolor*, manifesting potent words I needed to define and gloss for myself. I wasn't "bargaining" or "depressed"; I was holding onto my *herencia*, to what mis papas left behind, palabras worthy of my torment and pena. The words transported me into the past, where my pain was still present, and presente. Where the dolor is happening, right now.

> Recuerdo: (n.) memory, remembrance, recitation. From Latin *recordare*, *re (*new) + cordis (*corazón/* heart), as in "to return to the heart" or "to know by heart," attributed to ancient beliefs that the heart was the seat of the mind.

It is 5PM. My sister and I sit in the front seat and watch Papi carefully to make sure he is not jarred by the bumpy streets and turns the car makes. He is covered in a blanket. The blue one he always liked.

Papi is tired and pale in the back seat. He looks out the window at the streets whirring by and I wonder what he is thinking. Is he wondering if he'll see these again? Does he appreciate the beauty? Is he hurt by the noise?

As we pull into the driveway, my mother comes out to give my dad a kiss. "¿Listo?"I ask Papi, getting ready to lift him from the car and carry him into the house.

"No," Papi says. "Me quedo aquí un rato."

My mother doesn't understand why he wants to stay in the car. "Por favor," she pleads. "It's cold out here."

"No," Papi replies. "Está fresco, y el viento . . . " he closes his eyes and I can feel the breeze across his eyelashes. I want to enjoy this for a moment, he says.

My mother sighs heavily, almost exasperated, but I know she's just worried. "Te traigo un Ensure," she decides. What flavor do you want?

"Fresa," says my Papi, his eyes still closed. The autumn wind blows silkily through the car and he smiles gently.

I sit with him after my sister and mother go inside. The sky is orange like falling leaves, and the sun hides behind the hills. "Mira," my dad says. "Mira que bonito está la tarde."

"Sí," I agree. It *is* a beautiful evening.

We are quiet, enjoying the sounds of a day coming to a close. Cars motor by, coming home to almost-ready dinners, and children finish a soccer game in the street. Some neighbors open their garage doors and we hear the clink of tools and metal. In the distance, the steady sound of trains rolling by.

My mother returns with the vitamin drink and tries to convince my father to come inside again. Papi shakes his head slightly. "Un poquito más," he says. My mother concedes and tells me to watch him. "Cuídalo," she pleads, her eyes tearing up as she passes me the drink.

Not much time is left, I suddenly realize. Ya casi.

I move from the passenger seat to the back with my dad. I put the straw to his lips and he drinks slowly, enjoying the strawberry taste and the coolness in his throat. He smiles again. "Qué rico," he whispers. "Es mi favorito."

I smile. It's my favorite flavor too.

The sky is now purple-red, and we are still sitting in the car. The blanket keeps Papi warm as the breeze turns cooler, and the strawberry smell is strong as night falls. Looking at my dad, my heart quickens and breaks. I wish I could take him to Disneyland, or the park, to the grocery store or the library, anywhere, but he can't. There will be no more trips, big or small; no random outings; no more pondering an evening's beauty. I will sit alone in the car.

My heart will beat alone.

But for now, I enjoy this moment. The sounds of the street, the sun setting—this is all he needs to know that he is alive. All Papi needs to feel this day is worth living.

He closes his eyes and the light of his smile shines. His beauty is blinding and intense, but I will not turn away. I will look, and look, and look, recording every glimmer until I can't see him anymore.

Tormenta: (n.) the inflicting of torture; a state of great suffering and distress; meteorological phenomenon produced by violent winds, rains, and lightning. From Latin *tormentum*: "twisted cord, instrument of torture," from Indo-European *terkw*, to twist.

My mom was finally released after 36 days in the ICU. We began the day near Downtown LA and ended it at a clinic in West Covina, and that place was horrible: cold, colorless, the staff nothing like the family we'd made at the ICU. All of those nurses, aides, physical therapists, interns, surgeons, cooks and cashiers, everyone had our familia Bracho in action. We made them part of the family because we needed them to understand the value of someone like Leonor Bracho. Why someone like her needed to stay alive.

On her last day, the new attending physician in the cardiothoracic ICU was Dr. West. He smiled a lot and used soft platitudes as he explained my mom's case during 7AM rounds that morning. Dr. West wasn't ready for my interrogation, not realizing I'd been there every day, nearly twelve hours a day, for those other thirty-five days. I knew her telemetry, her blood pressure, her cardiac index, the number of CCs of urine in her failing kidneys, the settings to her respirator and dialysis machine. Dr. West was new to the situation, and quickly realized that my mom had been so traumatized after thirty-five days, that she just wanted him to release her, without questions, as we had all been planning for days with the last physician, Dr. Klein.

It was time. She was ready. There would be no more negotiations.

So, the next ten hours became all about disconnecting my mom from the various gadgets and machines that were keeping her little body going. The IVs were detached, her tracheostomy was cleaned up, the feeding tube was removed, her wounds freshly dressed. Throughout, my mom sustained a face of miserable dignity, enduring prods and pokes by random characters who appeared and disappeared in a flurry of activity. Forms signed, data shared, long-term plans confirmed and catalogued. My mom took it all in as if detached from her own future. She could not sit up on her own, breathing was ragged, her kidneys were parched, and she could not speak. On every front, her body was wrecked. Failing.

After seeing my mother transported to the ambulance, I got in my car and felt a sense of resolve as I followed it down the 10 East. I dared to feel optimistic, affirming that I would get up the next morning and begin the next phase with her. We would make this acute care clinic work for her, and I was committed to spending as many hours as I could there. I envisioned when my new job began in a few weeks, I would go to campus to teach, but not bother with meetings or office hours. What mattered was getting through my classes and coming back to my mamita. I imagined eating a quick breakfast in the morning, having coffee at the clinic as I sat with her, rushing home during lunch, making another visit before heading to my evening classes, and then stopping by on the way home. I mentally sorted the potential surgeries she might need to have, considered the therapy she'd have to endure, enumerated the ways I would support her, and love her, and be present, through all those moments in the months ahead.

I did not know that when I left the clinic that night, my mom would be gone six hours later.

In that state of ignorant bliss, I took a long shower, ordered a hamburger, got on the phone with my girl Nicole. We chatted and drank wine; I relaxed. I felt a huge obstacle had been overcome. We had left the ICU. My mother was *alive*. She was going to make it. I knew it was true, because I had pleaded with her longtime doctor, Dr. Michaels, to be real with me that last week at the ICU. *Is my mom going to survive this? Is she really going to bounce back?* Yes, he said, and he sounded so sure of himself that I foolishly believed him.

Around 2AM, I woke up in a state of terrified confusion. I sensed something was wrong immediately, and then saw dozens of missed calls from my sisters and brothers. I redialed my sister Lizzette. "She didn't make it," she announced sadly, quietly, not able to say hello. "She didn't make it."

I howled then, a cry in my gut that had been forming for weeks, months, even years, finally erupting, a shriek that felt unstoppable. I writhed around my apartment in a frenzy, shouting "No!" and "Mamita!" into my phone. My neighbors probably thought I was being murdered.

About twenty minutes later, I was at the clinic, and saw cousins and in-laws leaving her room, a sight that made me furious. Why the hell had other people been allowed to see my mom before me? Why did they have the right to see her before me? Why had I slept through all those fucking calls?

The sudden rabia came and went in a matter of seconds. I entered her room, fell to my knees by the low bed, and sobbed. Her eyes were closed, her mouth shut, in a frozen look that somehow still radiated warmth, and peace. I held her hand, I thanked her for her life. I let go of the day, a day that had begun with a hope, that maybe, deep down, I knew was just a dream.

Now, that dream was over. She was gone.

Fallecer: (v). To die. A euphemism in Spanish, from Latin *fallere*: to fail; to deceive; to cause to fall. Related: Old French *falir*, "not succeed; run out, come to an end."

I am back there again, now, in his room. It's Saturday, and Papi is on hospice care which means he will go any day. The nurse has left and it is early evening—about 5PM.

I don't know it, but this will be the last time I speak to my father.

He is curled in the bed. The TV burns bright, and his reflection in the closet mirror reminds us all he is dying. The smell of medicine pervades every molecule of the room. Morbidly, I think that with each breath I am inhaling a bit of my father's body. A bit of his death.

Papi's eyes are sunken, yellow with disease, as he turns to me slightly and sees the book I am holding. *Introducing Chaos*, it announces. "¿Qué es?" he asks.

I attempt to explain chaos theory in my pocho Spanish. I stumble over the words and try to tell my father why a butterfly flapping its wings in Brazil can cause a hurricane in Texas. A gleam in the corner of his eye tells me he knows what I am really trying to say, but he doesn't say much.

Sitting there, I realize that it will be soon. When my sister comes in to clean his bed wound, the lightness, frailty, and decay of his body tell us as much. This is a body that will not last. This is a body that will soon give in. When he dies, his molecules will spiral out into the universe, to reside in the water that I drink, the air that I breathe, the blankets that I sleep in.

This is the chaos we live in. The order of things.

The machine drips more morphine into his line and my father's eyes become glazed and sleepy. I keep talking as he drifts into sleep. I stroke his hand and feel the rise of his veins, the valley of his palm. His skin against my skin and his raspy breath are all I feel.

Papi is slipping away and becoming an angel, and as he flaps his wings a hurricane forms in my soul.

Resignación: (n.) permitting something following resistance;

action of returning a charge, abdicating a symbol of power.
From Latin *re-* (backward), *signare* (make a sign, mark, print).

The night after my mom died, we all gathered at the house. There wasn't anywhere else I could imagine being that night, the place where my parents raised five kids, tended to dogs, birds, and gardens. I felt lost and only my house could comfort me.

My cousins and tíos arrived at some point, along with some of mami's friends, and the house was full of noise. Overwhelmed, I burst into tears at one point, and my cousin came over to me. Don't cry primo, she insisted, she's at peace! Someone else told me to stop crying because I was making him want to cry. Angry, I left the crowd and retired to my mom's room. I sat on her bed and suddenly decided that this is where I would spend the night. The place where I would spend the first full night in the world without her.

I slept heavy. I voyaged through a dark void without images, but the sound of a rooster crowing woke me up around 5AM, a sound I recognized from my childhood. Laying inside her blankets, I felt a sense of bliss; I could smell her there still, that sweet scent of lotion and perfume. I lingered awake for a bit before drifting into sleep again.

In this dream, I walked through her bedroom to the little attached room I used when home from school. I even lived in it for a year, with my mom and I living like roommates in a sitcom. As I crossed her room, I looked over to the bed—the same bed on which I was asleep—and saw her there. She wore one of her casual, cozy PJs that she liked, a light pink smock, and sat cross-legged, as she always did while flicking through her Facebook page and watching something terrible like *Hoarders*.

But in this dream, there was no tablet, no TV. Just her, beaming at me, a bright light all around her as she gave me that smile I had seen thousands of times in my life. A look of pure love, a look that told me she knew my heart, my goodness; a look that radiated pride that I was her child. In that dream, I basked and bathed in her light, knowing she was no phantom.

It was her, come to say goodbye.

Two weeks later, at the funeral, hundreds of people showed up to pay their last respects, and many of her amigas stopped to chat with me. More than once, a señora would say to me, espero que pronto te llegue la resignación, a phrase that irritated me after days of being told I shouldn't cry, or that she was in a better place. Resignation? I wondered. How the hell would I ever want to feel that?

Five years later, I finally understand. In English, resignation means giving up, but I think in Spanish it's about giving *in*: not accepting, but *allowing*. I do not feel resignation, but I do feel resignación: the ability to resign, to flip the meaning of things. In writing about how my parents fallecieron, I recognized I was not experiencing "grief," but dolor. I was not "angry," I was spiraling in a tormenta; not "depressed," but lost in recuerdos. Grieving in Spanglish, within two herencias, two tongues.

My dolor is pulchritudinous: a word that sounds ugly, but actually means beautiful. It is a displaced love for my beloved mom and dad that I keep making a place for, a recuerdo engraved in my heart, a love I will not let go.

I will not grieve so as to complete a cycle. I will not accept anything.

Instead, me resigno: I re-sign myself, making new meanings rather than accept old ones. I find words to match my Spanglish DNA. I unearth gems that take me backward and forward through time, to all my beautiful dolores, eternally.

HEALING
MAKING OURSELVES WHOLE

for when our blood runs   motherless

Gisselle Yepes

today I put water on our altar weep   *Wela bendición* like Wela
        please come to this room in Indiana in a state you've
never been like Wela I miss you   I learned water has no enemy
like water a portal   between
us like yes I know milk spoils so I bring you a glass of peace
mirrored   today I place a glass of water on our altar
today your coffee is dark for the first time   leaves soil circled
on its rims   when you drink today   I remember how you
drank your coffee light and sweet   had cabinets
full of mugs and drank coffee in a tomato paste
metal can and you   peeled its skin sleeved
your nails tearing and you poured coffee
and we worried about your lips   how blood tastes like metal
how metal will sharpen its teeth   to look for blood today
I make soup that needs   tomato paste   so I reach
for a can filled   place a tool at its teeth to open its mouth   and
I   bleed today
I cry on our altar which is also   our kitchen
how close you were to hurting
yourself   a can of aluminum rimming   your teeth
today I break   all of our mugs   in the sink   how useless
everything feels   when we try   to keep our mothers alive
like we watched   you try to breathe   masked with oxygen
and nothing changed   except that you were dying
today I cry   in our kitchen singing today I am alive and
maybe I am motherless so I sit   on the floor of our altar and
weep   once I'd sit on floors and look for glass
to rim   skin   today I drink   water and do not look
in the mirror   the last time   I looked

I noticed my neck   pulsing   and remembered her neck
trying   gasping   to breathe   so I cry faced down
on the earth   which is   also our altar and o   how I weep
how we tried so hard   to keep her   alive
how she wanted   to die   for so long and I
understand   like there is glass shattered   in the sink
which looks   like teeth

How Latin Trap Helped Me Heal From the Biggest Romantic Heartbreak of My Life

Raquel Reichard

At a crowded hookah lounge in Downtown Orlando, where my girlfriends briefly whisk me away from post-breakup anguish, an opening G note played on a piano pulsates through the speakers. Immediately, I blow mango-mint smoke into the hazy room and pass the hose off, ready to replace pain with *perreo*.

Paso mucha' noches pensándote/Yo no sé ni cómo, ni cuándo fue

The keys lift me up from the seat I made for myself on a large windowsill at the back of the bar.

Pero sólo sé que yo recordé/cómo te lo hacía yo aquella vez

I shout each word passionately to my homegirls who yell them back, our acrylic nails pointing at each other like handguns as we ignite the dancefloor with each heated blast.

Y yo no puedo seguir solo pero sé/ que te boté

Throwing my hips back with my derrière perched in the air, Ozuna's voice booms.

De mi vida te boté, y te boté/ Te di banda y te solté, yo te solté/ Pa'l carajo usté' se fue, y usté' se fue/ De mi vida te boté, yo te boté

I bend, sway, bounce, clap, squat, shake and repeat. I've experienced this same moment numerous times in the last year: in Cuba, where I got my groove back grinding to the breakup hit at a Havana nightclub; at a Bad Bunny concert in New York, when my friend recorded and sent a clip of me shaking my ass to the Latin trap king himself while he performed it onstage; in Puerto Rico, during an actual "perreo sucio en La Placita"; and in my bedroom, where I spent the most time dancing through grief and healing through music.

In the year since my ex-boyfriend of eight years and I parted ways, music, particularly the rhythms and rhymes of Latin trap and reggaeton jams, have supported me. Songs like the energetic Nio Garcia and Casper Magico's "Te Bote" remix, featuring Bad Bunny, Ozuna and Nicky Jam, offered me an escape when the agony felt overwhelming. But El Conejo Malo's emo refrains and Karol G's self-assured hooks also helped me confront my oscillating emotions when I was ready, comforted me when I needed to cry, thumped my chest when I was angry, returned my confidence when I felt worthless and, ultimately, helped heal my shattered heart.

The resurgence of urbano music to the mainstream, by way of 2017 bangers like Natti Natasha and Ozuna's "Criminal," Karol G and Bad Bunny's "Ahora Me Llama" and, of course, Luis Fonsi and Daddy Yankee's "Despacito," has coincided with my own returning. This was the year my tumultuous relationship reached its end. The healthy and happy bond my ex and I created started chipping away two years earlier, but love, and perhaps habit, kept us fighting an unwinnable, destructive battle. We were both to blame. One's infidelity, the other's selfishness, one's depression, the other's lack of support, our mutual loss of respect. We kissed and said goodbye on July 4, my very own Independence Day.

It was cordial, with us laughing in a rented car he drove from our apartment in Washington, D.C., to my new home on my best friend's couch in Queens, but rage and despair still pulsated in both of our bodies. "Why couldn't you love me enough to change," he roared on late-night phone calls. "Why couldn't you love me enough to stay," I'd fire back. Away from each other, where we were no longer able to physically comfort one another through the pain we were guilty of causing, anger brewed, boiled and erupted. Irate one summer morning, I put my headphones on and started jogging at a neighborhood park.

Salí jodido la última vez que en alguien yo confié/ Me compré una forty, y a Cupido se la vacié

Bad Bunny's baritone pounded into my ears, both fueling and validating my wrath.

No me vuelvo a enamorar, no/ No me vuelvo a enamorar

In my feelings, I shouted with the Puerto Rican rapper, prompting stares from Little Leaguers at baseball practice and a group of elder Asian women performing their morning Tai Chi.

Sigue tu camino que sin ti me va mejor/ Ahora tengo a otras que me lo hacen mejor/ Si antes yo era un hijo de puta, ahora soy peor/ Ahora soy peor, ahora soy peor, por ti

The truth: I didn't have other lovers, and I preferred the heartbreak to turn me into a better partner, not a worse one, but El Conejo Malo's 2017 salty breakup jam "Soy Peor" allowed me to experience, vicariously, all the irrational, not-so-healthy post-separation episodes that outrage leads to without actually doing them and regretting it later.

Even more, songs like Chris Jeday's lovers-turned-foes beef track "Ahora Dice," featuring J. Balvin, Ozuna and Arcángel, and Bunny's fuck love anthem "Amorfoda" legitimized my feelings. I was angry at myself, at him, and at all the promises we made to each other and plans we had for the future. I was regretful, for the ways I didn't show up for him that I should have, for accepting behaviors and situations that I wasn't OK with, and for subscribing to bullshit societal standards of romantic relationships. I was done with trying to make something work that wasn't serving either of us, with romantic love and with ruminating on all of it.

I wasn't well at all—and I needed, for my own physical safety and mental stability, to feel whole again, to feel like me again, to feel loved again. So I left my job and industry opportunities to head back home to Orlando, where I found comfort, understanding, and warmth in family and lifelong friends. Surrounding myself with the unconditional love of a nephew's laugh, a niece's beg to play, a mother's midnight head massages and a father's weekly pep talks, it was hard to be angry. For a while, that ire transformed into longing, a yearning for the good ol' times, before disappointment turned to rage and led to betrayal.

High off some kush in the backseat of a car, I'm in my feelings.

Tal vez no te pienso pero no te olvido/Tal vez yo te extraño pero no lo digo

Bryant Myers' tenor has me on a long-avoided trip down memory lane.

Tal vez no cumplí nada de lo que juré/Tal vez tus heridas nunca las curé

Once traveling on this slippery road, it's difficult to steer back to my path of healing. Myers' not-quite-over-you banger "Triste" featuring Bad Bunny has me in my head, unable to focus on the present because I realize I'm not yet over the past. I create a *sad girl* playlist, with Ozuna's "Farsante" forcing me to reconsider if the freedom that comes from singlehood really is as appealing as Bunny told me it was, and Benito Antonio Martínez Ocasio's own "Dime Si Te Acuerdas" reminding me of "*to' lo* que *hacíamos hasta* que saliera *el sol.*"

My mood is heavy again, and my girlfriends take notice. They see me prioritizing my healing—journaling and meditating to identify where I contributed to the demise of this relationship, trying to understand why, holding myself accountable, forgiving us both, and trying to become a stronger and better me at the end—but they stress that I also need to make space for joy during this emotional journey. I heed their advice.

Yo la conozco a ella es reservá'/Nunca ha salió' con un extraño/Pero esta noche está revelada/por culpa de un bobo que le hizo daño

Real Hasta La Muerte blares from my bestie's car speakers as we head downtown, eager to dance our woes away for a night.

Ella quiere beber, ella quiere bailar/Su novio la dejó y lo quiere olvidar/Ella se entregó y el tipo le falló y por eso se va a rumbear

Tonight, smutty *trapero* Anuel AA is encouraging me to bust out of my timid confines and let the champagne and club beats help me forget the one who broke my heart, even if just for a few hours. Next week, when I'm in Miami for a five-day getaway with two other homegirls who are fresh out of relationships, it's Ozuna's "Se Preparó" urging us to dry our tears and doll ourselves up for a night on the dance floor.

These frequent reggaeton parties aren't mending my broken

heart alone—my ongoing self-awareness and self-care practices are doing most of that work—but they are helping me regain a confidence in myself that I thought was gone forever and allowing me to discover a sexy that I never even knew existed.

Pero tú 'ta grande, 'ta madura/Pasan los años y te pones más dura

I take a sip of champagne between laughs as Bad Bunny sings through a speaker in my hotel room, where I celebrated my 28th birthday last July.

Baby, cómo te cura/Mientras me tortura

Cosculluela's "Madura," which features Benito, feels like it was recorded with me and this day in mind. Here I am, another year older and feeling badder than ever in my low-cut, skintight, thunder-thighs-baring little black dress, and one year out of the longest and most pivotal romantic relationships of my life, maturing and healing in ways that were unimaginable 365 days prior.

That has been Latin trap and reggaeton's greatest gift to me throughout my heartbreak: reminding me of who the fuck I am. When I hear Melii rap, *"Tú me tienes tema / Cuida'o, si me tocas, te quemas"* in her bilingual bop "Icey," my insecurities trickle away and are replaced with self-assuredness. When Natti Natasha sings, *"Cuidao, las mujeres tienen poder"* in Daddy Yankee's "Dura" remix, featuring la baby de urbano, Bad Bunny and Becky G, I'm reminded of my own enduring power. When Anitta croons, *"En las noches soy yo la que define/ todo a lo que vá a pasar. / A mí no me tienes que mandar"* in her tantalizing Spanish-language hit "Downtown" featuring J Balvin, I, too, feel sexy and comfortable making demands in the bedroom. With this renewed confidence, I'm now able to recognize, for the first time, the treasures that come with a single life.

Ahora me llama/diciendo que le hago falta en su cama

My phone rings. It's yet another FaceTime call from my ex, the third this week.

Sabiendo que eso conmigo no va, ya no va/Ahora solo quiero salir con mi propia squad

I pick up. It's all love, always and forever, but that doesn't mean either of us want to rekindle this flame.

Es porque la noche es mía/La voy a disfrutar sin tu compañía

Life is the best it's been in months, probably years. I'm not as stressed these days, so my skin is clear and my hair can easily land a spot in a shampoo commercial. I do what I want to do when I want to do it, whether that's cozy solo nights in watching Netflix or catching a last-minute arena game with a homegirl. My money is mine, and I spend it traveling the globe and investing in my future. As Karol G sings in her chart-topper "Ahora Me Llama," "*Yo soy dueña de mi vida. A mi nadie me manda.*"

After spending eight years with someone who I once considered the love of my life, many of them beautiful yet others painfully tumultuous, I'm at a place, post-anger and post-despair, where I'm learning what it's like to be alone, particularly as an adult. It's an opportunity I never had before, and I'm surprisingly enjoying it. But I'm aware that this solitude won't last forever. My "Amorfoda" "fuck love" stage is behind me. My heart isn't cold. Instead, I'm excited to love and care again. After all, that's when my Cancer spirit feels its best. But before that day comes, I'm savoring, and being intentional about, these moments—my time with and for me.

Today, at the start of a new year and almost two years single, I'm feeling a bit like the *trapero* who has been with me throughout my heartbreak, Bad Bunny, in his debut album *X100PRE*: "Ni Bien Ni Mal."

Her·me·neu·tics

Edyka Chilomé

noun
    1. the branch of knowledge that deals with interpretation, especially of the Bible or literary texts.

I begin by admitting that this language is proof of my drifting.
A testimony of my involuntary deviation and instinctual navigation.
They have called me poet,
                a charge not a choice,

a.designation of spirit independent of any word written or spoken
because what is this language if not proof of my poverty? Proof of
separation? Proof of displacement? What is this language if not
proof of my courage? Proof of resilience, mala yerba, territorio
salvaje,   chilomé.

What am I but proof of a grueling encounter grown in the captivity of chaos,
the magnificent and miraculous alchemy of survival.

I have chosen liberation by way of its cartography,
            awakened by its intoxicating translations of life.

These words weave what so many of our grandmothers weaved
with their hands and their mourning hearts: Story. Map. Prayer.
Song. Poem.   The way home.

It is all we have and at this point it is all we have come to know.

Because what is life but a whole ass love poem.

Pa'lante Moments

Claude M. Bonazzo-Romaguera

I believe the first time I started using pa'lante moments was when my mom completed her last round of chemo for breast cancer. It was a big day because she would no longer have to do chemo and we thought it would start a new phase in her life. Our family put personal messages on pink hearts that were taped onto the garage door so that the first thing she saw when she got home were words of celebration from family members. On Facebook, I posted 'Mom's Pa'lante Moment' with pictures of the hearts and of family members who shared that day with her. About a month later, I completed four hours of testing on my eyes to determine what kind of vision therapy I needed to do in the years ahead. This was shortly after my fifth muscle eye surgery to correct my double vision. In a way, pa'lante moments emerged from the struggles of my mom with breast cancer and my struggle to correct my double vision. Life takes time and we should always celebrate the small wins along the way. I call these pa'lante moments.

Pa'lante is a common phrase we use in Puerto Rico, it is short-hand for "para adelante" meaning "forward." It is commonly used among my family when we encounter a difficult life event or obstacle, pa'lante would motivate us to continue to move forward. Furthermore, the Young Lords, a Puerto Rican civil rights activist group, used the phrase as the title of their movement newspaper starting in the 1960s. In many ways, it was a rallying cry for the once street gang turned political movement. These are the social and cultural seeds which pa'lante moments stem from and are the building blocks from which I have developed this practice.

Trying to handle the stress of my mom's cancer, my double vision, my cognitive disability, and raising a newborn child all while pursuing my PhD was incredibly overwhelming. At the time, I began to have panic attacks on a regular basis. I decided one day to go to the counseling and mental health center at the university and make an appointment with a therapist. It was during my first appointment my therapist introduced me to mindfulness. Throughout the session, I explained all of the stressors and difficulties in my life to my therapist. I began to get emotional and even started to cry. The therapist paused the session, and we did a short mindful breathing exercise. I began to feel a little better. She talked about a mindfulness meditation group that met weekly for sessions to help support this practice.

The more I learned about mindfulness and meditation, the more I became fascinated in learning about the brain and the mind. I found hope in the idea that I can be part of the antidote to my own suffering. I felt empowered to learn the source and essence of my anxiety. I began to realize my anxiety stemmed from my fixation on all the possible negative outcomes for myself and my mom. The possibility of never being able to see single again and not completing my doctoral program made me feel hopeless. The possibility that I might lose mi mamá was crushing.

Most of the research on mindfulness demonstrates real changes in the brain and the body. When I told my good friend Marian about what I was doing to overcome anxiety and stress, she suggested I read the book *Train Your Mind, Change Your Brain: How a New Science Reveals Our Extraordinary Potential to Transform Ourselves* by Sharon Begley. This book introduced me to the current research on meditation and its real potential to transform our minds. The Dalai Lama and a group of leading Western scientists addressed the question "Is it really possible to change the structure and function of the brain, and in so doing alter how we think and feel?" The research was indicating "that we all have the power to literally change our brains by changing our minds."[1] I came to my own profound realization that I can be the antidote to my own mind!

One day, when I was in the copy room making copies of an exam, I had a chance encounter with a wonderful and kind professor in the department. I just had my second brain surgery to replace my shunt and there were a bunch of staples on my head. The professor asked me what happened. I told her that I had two brain surgeries to replace my shunt, that I had experienced some pretty serious complications as a result of the first surgery

---

1 Begley, Sharon. 2007. *Train Your Mind, Change Your Brain: How a New Science Reveals Our Extraordinary Potential to Transform Ourselves*. New York: Ballantine Books.

which necessitated the second one. This kind professor, showing a great deal of compassion and kindness, said "I am so sorry you went through this difficult moment." I quickly responded "It is okay. I have had many surgeries in my life. I am used to it. I am glad it was me and not someone else. I wouldn't want anybody to go through that." She responded "Wow, you have the bodhisattva attitude. You are describing your experience as someone who practices tonglen." Tong means "sending," and len means "taking." It is essentially the exchanging of oneself with others by taking in the pain and suffering of others and sending out whatever will benefit others. It is a Buddhist technique to develop compassion and loving kindness for ourselves and others.

I wanted to learn more! I asked if we could meet and talk more, and she said yes. I went to her office and told her about how I was becoming really interested in Buddhism. She suggested a new book, at the time, that had recently come out called *How to Be Sick: A Buddhist-Inspired Guide for the Chronically Ill and Their Caregivers* by Toni Bernhard. This was a crucial moment for me. For almost five years I had been struggling with double vision and the stress associated with it. I could not drive from home to campus which was about a thirty to forty-five-minute drive. I ended up having to commute by bus which increased the commute time. Time away from my family. Having double vision made seeing incredibly difficult. It was especially difficult trying to complete readings for my graduate coursework and dissertation.

I asked if there was a Buddhist community I could join to further study Buddhism and its practices. Out of her compassion to help she invited me to her Discovering Buddhism study group. This started my wonderful journey to learn about Buddhism and its many practices to help cultivate happiness and compassion for self and others.

The idea of pa'lante moments emerged as a combination of Buddhist philosophy and psychology with my Puerto Rican roots and culture. Buddhism was teaching me that happiness is a skill, it does not just happen to you. It is a slow and meticulous process of understanding your mind and identifying the sources of your suffering and finding your sources of happiness and joy. Each of us creates our own realities and how we respond to the social world around us. The person you find beautiful may be seen by someone else as ugly. The food you enjoy and look forward to eating may be viewed with disgust by someone else. Buddhism stresses that it is important to become familiar with your own mind. The Tibetan word for "to meditate" is *gom* which directly translates as "to familiarize." It also emphasizes the importance of creating positive states of mind. Our brains are hardwired with a negativity bias that stems from our evolutionary tendency to see potential threats in order to survive.

As for Puerto Rican influences, pa'lante meant to keep moving forward in the face of adversity. This was a phrase I frequently heard among family, friends, and people in my community. Because I was going through my own adversity with my vision and my mom's fight with breast cancer, I began to learn that I had a choice to either focus on the negative or positive moments. I chose to focus on the small moments or steps that led us both to the path of being well again.

Overcoming adversity is not solely when you have achieved the desired outcome or goal, it is all the little steps you took to get you there. The little wins are a part of your journey. Anybody who plays sports knows that they failed many times before they became successful in a particular move or skill. Once they accomplished a particular skill they would move on to the next and start the process again. If we don't recognize these moments, we miss out on all the causes and conditions that led us to our goal. Our hard work. The support of our loved ones. The kindness of others. We are an interconnected and interdependent species. Many little things had to come together to make you who you are today.

The primary source of my pain during this time of learning about mindfulness and developing what I would come to call pa'lante moments were my experiences while pursuing a PhD. I attended one of the top public universities in the country. I had only applied to one PhD program because I did not want to move my wife and son to another state. The first year I applied I was rejected. I decided to figure out what exactly the department was looking for and why I did not get in. My GRE scores were not great largely since I was unable to get extra time on the exam because of my disability. I also had difficulty with the vocabulary section since I grew up learning both Spanish and English. I don't know how many times I would get called out for not knowing difficult words or even sayings. When you focus on learning just one language it is easier to garner more depth in vocabulary and idioms. The GRE only measured my strength in the English language and not my strength of knowing two languages.

After visiting the department a number of times for events, I was able to make some connections that helped strengthen my application to get in the program. I developed a wonderful relationship with a man who was Puerto Rican and Mexican. I felt I could relate with him more because of our shared backgrounds. He was kind enough to mentor me through my application process the second time. I applied again and got in.

Once enrolled, the first thing I did was register with Services for Students with Disabilities, the office that provided accommodations for students with disabilities. In the past, I had gotten extra time on exams and assignments. But when I signed up for accommodations in graduate school there were really no accommodations for students in PhD programs. In PhD programs there is less structure compared to high school and my undergraduate experience. You were expected to focus on your own performance. Some of the possible accommodations that would have helped my experience in the graduate program would have been to add extra time to complete the program and additional funding. The general timeline to complete a PhD is five to six years. I completed my program in eight years. I was on the verge of getting kicked out.

Another possible accommodation would be a reduced course load that was available at the undergraduate level but not at the graduate level because of funding. I was supported by a very prestigious institution and one of the requirements was I had to take nine credit hours every semester. Graduate school is a very elite space that is centered on the best, brightest, and quick-witted. Many programs don't believe students with disabilities can or should be in their programs, let alone a Puerto Rican with a disability.

For some professors, it felt strange to give me more time on papers and exams because the academic environment was a space that focused on students with some of the top qualifications in the country. I think this strangeness for professors originated from their experience in the academic world and being one of the top universities and by design only the best and brightest would enter the world of academia or from their own ableist perspectives. For them, the "best and the brightest" could by definition not include folx with a disability. They expect everyone's brain/body to work exactly the same while knowing fully well that this is just not true.

This was an elite space. In other words, as Nirmal Puwar puts it, I was a space invader because of my disability and being Latinx. Luckily, there were other Latinx people in the department that I naturally gravitated toward, and this made me feel at home. Speaking Spanish with colleagues from Latin America and hanging out with others who were marginalized helped me feel like I was not alone. They helped me ground myself back to who I really was as a Boricua.

On top of these difficulties, my wife and I had just had our first child and we essentially lived off student loans. I would work as a graduate research assistant during the day and in the evening my wife would work overnight shifts at a children's hospital as a Spanish interpreter. The financial stress, marital strain, graduate school, and the need to provide a stable home for our child was overwhelming and exhausting. Furthermore, I had several personal medical issues pop up during the program, two brain surgeries to replace my shunt. Three corrective eye muscle surgeries to correct my double vision along with five years of vision therapy. Between the surgeries and therapy, it felt like I never had time to just live a "normal" life and complete the graduate program.

The illnesses of my mom and my dad further intensified my stress and anxiety. My mom fought breast cancer for a year. I drove frequently from Austin to Houston to go to my mom's major appointments and to some of her chemo treatments. After a year of treatments, we celebrated the first pa'lante moment at our house. I even have pictures from that day. It felt like we could finally move on with our lives. Shortly after it was discovered that she had lymphoma. Her body had been through so much physically and mentally that her immune system had been compromised and she developed a second form of cancer. Unfortunately, the outlook was not good.

In the following months, my mom went through a number of different treatments and surgeries to stop the lymphoma. Our family was told that she may not survive. I stopped the PhD program and went to help care for my mom. During these months I helped her to the shower and stood by the door to make sure she did not fall because of the neuropathy she developed from chemo.

I would help her go to the bathroom and sometimes that turned into a whole thing. I remember a particular day when I got into an argument with my brother and sister about who should help her to the bathroom. My brother and sister said that it was inappropriate and demeaning to help my mom wipe after peeing or pooping citing gender norms. My mom turned around and screamed "Callate la boca. Dejalo que lo haga. El sabe lo que esta haciendo!" which means "Shut your mouths. Let him do it. He knows what he is doing!"

Other times I would help rub lotion on her legs to help deal with the neuropathy and slept on a futon in her room to keep her company and make sure nothing happened overnight. I would also drive my mom to her many appointments for her treatments. We would sing ABBA songs from the movie *Mamma Mia!* during the drive. We would sing "Super Trouper" in particular. She had some pa'lante moments during her lymphoma treatment, but her body could not take it anymore. She died months later.

Even though she had many pa'lante moments she did not survive. I still consider her my Super Trouper. Reflecting on all these beautiful moments I had with her, I realize now that caring for my mom was a pa'lante moment in and of itself. It helped me come to terms with her difficult journey. It helped me see the joy and beauty of caring for my mom in her final moments in the world. It helped me more than anything to overcome the pain of losing my mom so early in my life.

These small victories my mom made during her treatment for breast cancer and lymphoma are what inspired me to apply them to my wins with my illnesses and difficulties. We usually tend to focus on the end goal, in this case, being cancer free or no longer seeing double, but the journey is just as valuable.

The next year my dad developed an infection from complications of diabetes. He was in the hospital for three months to get the infection under control and had a second toe amputated. During this time, I would make frequent trips to Houston to go visit him. I really feared I would lose him as well or that he would lose part of his leg. He recovered from his illness, but he would frequently have to go back to the hospital because of complications with his diabetes.

All the while, I had continuously reminded myself I was not supposed to be in my elite PhD program. So many students from all over the country and the world who came from prestigious universities, had received awards, scholarships, performed incredibly well on the GRE, and simply had an advantage over me. I was in a basic demographic methods course and the professor was going around the entire room of about twenty students asking them each the various steps in a particular statistical technique. Every student was able to follow and understand the exercise. I was completely lost. When the professor got to me and asked what the following step was, I said to skip me because I was lost and did not understand the exercise. He then began to probe what I did not understand. Since I was so lost in the exercise, I could not even describe my confusion. Everyone in that room was staring at me and wondering why I could not answer the simple question. Eventually the professor moved on to the next student. Shortly after, I left to go the restroom and cried uncontrollably.

There were many other times that I felt inadequate. I had a cognitive disability that affected my short-term memory. At times, it would take me much longer to process information from a lecture or even from an article or book I was reading for graduate school. Many times, I could not find adequate words to express myself in class or in my writing. What amplified this inadequacy was also the notion of being a Latino who did not get his bachelor's and master's from a prestigious university. Not having an expansive vocabulary and not knowing particular idioms or sayings. Some would even go to the point of saying, "Oh, you don't know what that word means?" I even had one student in the program tell me while we were having coffee at a café that many of the other students in the cohort did not believe I was putting in the work needed in my classes and that I was not taking the program seriously. This was a particularly crushing moment for me. One of the students who I had gotten to know well was telling me essentially that I did not belong in the program.

My medical issues re-emerged in the second year of the program when my double vision began to return. I went to the neuro-ophthalmologist that had done surgery on my eyes three times shortly after recovering from my brain tumor. The doctor believed I needed surgery again. During my years in the program, I had another three eye muscle surgeries to try to correct the double vision. Although two of the surgeries did not correct the double vision at the beginning, I knew my doctor was doing her best. Along with these surgeries, I had five years of vision therapy. The vision therapy was not covered by insurance. I had to pay out of pocket with my student loans and credit cards. Even though I was going through all these difficulties, I began to see my own pa'lante moments. I think the catalyst for recognizing my pa'lante moments was during the times I began to see improvement in my vision or even from completing difficult and at times painful vision exercises that I would frequently get headaches from.

As I mentioned, pa'lante moments emerged from the constant roadblocks and challenges I faced during my time in graduate school and in my personal life. After going to the counseling center a number of times and really incorporating mindful techniques I began to realize I have a choice. I can either focus on the positive aspects of my journey or on how I have failed or how incapable I am in moving forward through these difficulties. I can be the antidote to my own suffering. It just takes practice and work on my own mind. I need to highlight more the small wins and victories through my difficulties. I always reminded myself of a Chinese proverb "A journey of a thousand miles begins with a single step." Each of these pa'lante moment steps are a part of my journey. I should celebrate the difficult journey and the wisdom it has given me.

Every time I had a surgery, I knew I was getting closer to single vision. The fact that I survived when my shunt failed, and they attempted to replace it two times. Not dying from severe hydrocephalus because my wife observed I was not myself. After the initial replacement of the shunt my wife noticed that I was not getting better, and I was acting almost like a zombie. She fought with the nurse and nurse practitioner to do something about my condition. She told them she would go to another hospital and consider suing the hospital for not addressing my issue. They proceeded to go back in and fix my shunt. This was a pa'lante moment. I consider getting through each of my three muscle eye surgeries as a pa'lante moment. When I got horrible headaches from doing intensive vision therapy exercises, I saw those as pa'lante moments. I would always recognize the small wins from getting through different stages of the PhD program, for example, getting a conditional pass on my comprehensive exams. Helping to complete a book with my mentor. I would post regularly on Facebook all the pa'lante moments that I could identify during this journey. Our society and media inundate our minds with the difficulties and horrors of the world but rarely identify the many positive moments in history. We are programmed to focus on the negative.

Acknowledging and embracing the pa'lante moments is critical. Now, I am not trying to simply ignore or minimize the very real challenges and obstacles people and communities face. As a sociologist, culture, structure, and power are exactly what we study as a discipline. However, am I going to respond from a place of anger because I encountered these difficulties? I choose to respond with patience and compassion. If I hold on to the anger for too long, it ends up hurting me and won't help me come up with solutions to help resolve these issues.

The more I incorporated pa'lante moments with Buddhist philosophy and psychology I began to create a sense of peace in my life. I was being compassionate with myself and others, which helped me move forward. Learning to always listen and support the students in the following cohorts through their difficulties helped further develop my compassion. I found real happiness in helping others find peace and their pa'lante moments even though I might not have referenced it that way. There are many stories during my time at university that really showed me the beauty of compassion and how that would lead to my own happiness and others. Understanding that my own happiness was tied to helping others essentially circled me back to what I had learned early in my life about the importance of apoyar uno al otro. It was already a part of my culture and my family in Puerto Rico. Compassion for others was already imprinted in my mind.

Pa'lante moments emerged from suffering and pain. What I decided to do with that suffering was up to me. I can either ruminate on the suffering that was happening to me and my loved ones or I can decide to bring myself to the present moment. The only moment that matters. Although I went through the pain of many surgeries and difficulties, I was able to see the many circumstances and people that helped me through this journey. I find joy and beauty in that. Even though it was difficult for me to watch my mom slowly decline, I was able to share many pa'lante moments with her: when she got through a surgery, completed her chemo, or when she didn't feel pain. I found a great deal of joy in those moments, and it gave me solace in the many ways I made her laugh and celebrate her pa'lante moments in her journey. Each moment in our lives is precious and so is our time with others. As you cannot change the past and you cannot predict the future, the best choice is pa'lante.

Pacienca: How Learning to Sew Helped Me Heal

Esperanza Luz

At first, I didn't want to walk in my school's graduation ceremony. My family had not made plans to attend. They were thousands of miles away, so I didn't see the point. I didn't arrange to pick up a cap or gown or attend any of the practices. That is, until I found the amber piece of cloth. Out of nowhere I began daydreaming of joining the pomp and circumstance, wearing a simple hand sewn halter top under black regalia. I imagined myself feeling happy, like the color yellow, once again. Then I remembered I had no sewing skills. Still, I felt a strong need to hold that bright scrap of fabric in my hands.

***

I'm not exactly sure at what age the insidious Storyteller began to visit my mind, if I had to guess, I'd say it happened right around the time my father left home. This Storyteller has been whispering words like "you are despicable, unworthy, slimy, vile, ugly, wretched," to me ever since I was a tiny human. The Storyteller made a home in my mind, maneuvering me like a puppet. Until one day, one of the puppet strings finally broke.

***

A few weeks before becoming a college graduate, my Storyteller urged me to accept a date with a man that I truly had no interest in. My gut kept screaming "SOMETHING IS NOT RIGHT," but my Storyteller kept silencing my intuition, while urging me to be overly polite, grateful, pretty, obedient, quiet. The first night I met this man, he beat my face with his open palm and poured the stench of unripe lime and beer into my body.

***

I was sexually assaulted by a college alumni weeks before my graduation. Ironically, in the end, it was this trauma that motivated me to attend the ceremony. Although my family wasn't going to be there, I needed to be there for myself, for the little person who was first taken hostage by the Storyteller. I wore a borrowed black dress and my beaded Wirárika necklace and sat through that uncomfortably long ceremony. The person who assaulted me also attended the ceremony. When I saw him, my heart stopped. I darted through the crowds of happy, cheering families to avoid his gaze. I wanted so badly to feel proud of myself that day, but I mostly felt ashamed.

***

I am infinitely grateful for the few good friends who helped me escape. After the ceremony, they drove me to a nearby reservoir in the woods to swim. Floating belly up on the calm water, surrounded by evergreen trees, sun on my cheeks, I felt a simple kind of happiness, a yellow kind of happiness, one that I hadn't felt in a long while. Nature remains the holiest of healers in my life, calling me back to a truer version of myself again and again. Water, in particular, is an excellent teacher in non-resistance. For the first time in weeks, I felt assured that I would not drown.

***

I was drawn to that thrown-away, piece of amber colored cloth because it reminds me of myself. Like its vibrant color, on good days I radiate. Like its gritty texture, I also tend to be guarded. *Who would throw this away?* I thought. Pulling the scrap fabric out of the trash was a reminder that I still had the capacity to transform myself, create something beautiful, even if I didn't have all the skills right then. I knew I would need to learn how to sew, how to heal myself, if I was to bring this cloth's, my own, potential to fruition. In the end, I simply tucked this piece of fabric, this piece of me, away into a suitcase I sent home with all my warm sweaters.

***

When the pandemic finally hit the city I was living in, I made a spur of the moment decision to go back home to the Southwest to visit my mom. I only intended to stay for a couple of weeks, but time slipped and turned into three months. I cleaned out my childhood room, throwing away old shoes, and graded homework, and silly mementos. When I came across the piece of yellow textile again, I immediately remembered my daydream of sitting in front of a sewing machine and creating my own blouse. I asked my mother, "¿Me enseñas cómo usar tu máquina de coser?"

***

I was in the middle of completing the back of the blouse when the uprisings began. Gripped by outrage and hope, I decided to return to the city and redirect my creative energy. I hung the garment in my closet, knowing I was being pulled elsewhere, yet understanding it wouldn't be long before I would return to finish it.

***

When I returned to my mother's home for Christmas, I was determined to finish sewing the blouse. I completed the stitches in the back and sewed a small red button. When my mother saw me wearing it, a beautiful smile spread across her face, "No es perfecto, pero está bastante bien por no saber coser," she boastfully teased. You could tell she was proud to teach me how to sew, of co-creating this garment with me. I felt utmost gratitude for her patience in teaching me. Our exchange of words made it seem like the project had come to an end, but I still felt something was missing.

***

On the morning of Christmas Eve, my family and I sat together at the kitchen table drinking coffee and eating tamales, and somehow we began to discuss mental health. In that moment I found the courage to say it aloud, "I was sexually assaulted in my last month of college," and a single tear involuntarily rolled out of my eye. My brother, sister and mother listened sympathetically and asked questions in quiet voices. Unleashing this truth felt like a necessary purge, an enormous release. When I looked into my mother's crying eyes, I became suddenly, and inexplicably aware that my sexual trauma is not mine alone. My body carries a lineage, a memory, of women in my family who have suffered abuse. It was my older sister, who said what was happening in that moment, what I was feeling: *"This is healing."*

***

Paciencia.

***

In bright blue thread, I clumsily embroidered the word paciencia on the shirt. It now felt complete. More than a year had lapsed from the time I connected with that piece of fabric in the trash to the time I finished tying a knot on the final letter *a*. I created a physical, wearable, reminder that healing takes time, a lot of it. I am still healing and paciencia is the thread allowing me to transform generational pain into useful beauty.

andrea and i do shots over facetime

Gabriella Navas

tonight, she calls me during the pregame,
already two shots in. *do one with me,*
she giggles, and i have known her since
we were twelve years old so i say *of course.*
retrieve the bottle of bacardi i've hidden
in my sock drawer. i figure this is the closest
i'll get to being able to comfort her: to hold her
hand or curl up next to her like i did the last time
we drank together. i offer to get on the next bus out,
but she tells me she'll be fine. and i, like
i always do, believe her. because i have seen the
way she has healed from so much. because it is
our collective flaw to praise
someone's survival,
rather than to condemn the
suffering that requires it.
so we do another shot.
and now our throats are on fire
and we are
coughing up *i love you*s and laughing
because
we know how much our younger selves
would
judge us. how they'd fail to understand that,
sometimes, this is what solidarity looks like.
i start to wonder how many acts of care look
destructive on the surface. maybe every act
of care requires the destruction of something,
but tonight—tonight, we are only building.
tonight, this the ultimate *i got you, manita,*
and *i'm here till the sun burns out,* a *someday*
this pain won't be anything but a memory.
y te prometo que even if it changes you,
i'll still recognize you. siempre y por siempre.

After the Funeral

Yulissa Emilia Nuñez

It was a mayday tune. I am sure it annoyed some people, but the humming calmed me. With every vibration, I blocked out the sounds of people, my racing heart, my shaking legs, and the bewilderment at how I ended up in this situation.

My mother once told me that when I was a baby, my oldest sister and my grandmother fell in love with me and they pressured her to let me stay with them while my father was frantically trying to get me back to Massachusetts, where I was born. My mother was fighting with my father at the time and used me as leverage. To get back at him over whatever feud they had, I was not allowed to see him. I don't think I understood what it meant to have parents because I was left behind so young. Instead, I felt the love, guidance, and protection from my grandmother and extended family in the Dominican Republic. In the small town of Miches, way off in El Seibo province, I was raised with my six other siblings by my grandmother, Teresa. Many uncles, aunts, and cousins would stop by and stay with us too. Our house was big, and food would eventually appear from some source, later I would learn it was barely enough to go around. What I most loved about living there was the open space. My grandmother kept big white ducks and chickens, and there was plenty of room to run around and play with all my cousins. I loved traveling to the beach on foot and eating the fallen mangos.

My grandmother was a lovely woman, tough as nails with the purest of hearts. All my siblings, cousins, aunts, and uncles passed through my grandmother's hands, and every one of them has some hilarious story about her strict nature. She was a special lady to many, but she meant everything to me. I was traumatized when I was separated from her.

On the day of my flight, I remember a few things. Everyone

was friendly to me, and I liked the attention. I had two braided ponytails with bobble hair ties and a red cotton apple dress with green leaves. I do not remember my ride to the airport or when I said my goodbyes. I do not remember who I sat next to or what I did to pass the time.

I remember the humming.

Seven low, continuous hums replayed over and over. I remember the vibrations in my throat like a pulsating engine that clogged my ears, blocked my thoughts, and held back my tears. I did not know it then, but it was my distress call. I sent it the only way I knew how. Not a soul heard me. It sounded like an ambulance, a police cruiser, and a fire truck, all in one. It was a life-threatening emergency, and the only way to keep me alive was to return me to my grandmother.

For anyone on the island who must live with violence, poverty, a corrupt legal and political system, and a lack of resources and jobs, a move to the United States is the absolute best thing that could ever happen to a Dominican in the late 90s. Especially a child. They would not have to go through that form of pain and suffering. Everyone's dream was to make it out, to live in Nueva York making dolares even if it meant drowning on their way to Puerto Rico because they took a yola out of desperation. But I was just seven years old. I was too young to see the despair in people's eyes because I was happy, and that was all that mattered to me.

I cannot paint a complete picture of how my life was in Miches because my memories come in fragments. But, I can tell you how I felt. I never felt like I lacked something when staying with my grandmother. I never felt unloved. I never felt like a burden. I never felt like I was not capable of following my dreams. I never felt trapped. I was just a happy child who loved life very much.

My grandmother was always patient with me and did everything she could to make me feel safe, happy, and loved. With her, I felt like no matter how many times I messed up, I could always rely on her to be there without judgment. Sometimes I felt a deep rage and sadness inside me, and other times I felt bursts of excess energy. I broke a lot of things in the house—most of the time, by accident. I remember climbing up our wooden TV stand that held pictures of dead and living family members, saints, candles, and other decorative items while my grandmother was entertaining guests in the kitchen. I don't remember what I was trying to reach, but I'm sure I would have had a good explanation. Unfortunately, the explanation would not have justified the broken frames and damage I caused when the stand toppled over. When it came to punishments, I never felt like my grandmother didn't love me whether she threw a chancleta at me, hit me with a tree branch, had me sit on rice, or locked me up in the galleria with nothing to play with but my imagination, rocks, and ants. Everything I did, no matter how I saw it, had consequences. I grew up understanding law and order. I always remember my grandmother being fair, and I never questioned how much space I took up in her heart.

When I think of my grandmother, I think of home. I think of a deep pain I never got to address. When I came to the United States, I do not remember anyone sitting me down and walking me through the changes. I was plucked from one place and thrown in another without anyone noticing the damage it did to my psyche. I was a child. I was so lost and confused. I was hurt. I wondered why I was stripped from the only person I loved with all my heart. I did not understand the world at all. I knew it wasn't my fault, so I did not blame myself, but I did believe it happened because I was the easiest to cast aside.

When I got to Massachusetts in 1999, I learned to play along in school, acquired English, and worked hard to make it. I played basketball to distract myself and tell myself over and over that what happened made sense, it was all for the best. I did not know how to talk to my father. He was a stranger to me—a man who got drunk, puked, and had the worst case of diarrhea most nights. I do not think he knew how to speak to me either. He was happy to have his daughter in his life, and that was all that mattered to him. I am close to my father today, but it was just too much for me when I was little.

Elementary school was hard. I do not know what kind of student I was. I remember a little hill all the kids would run up and down for recess. I remember the sunlight hitting the trees and a mean old bald lady who always picked on me. I think she had cancer. I remember a library, running my fingers through stacks of books and sitting down to read as many *Goosebumps* and Judy Blume books as I could. I liked Harry Potter, too. I enjoyed reading so much as a child because I understood the fictional worlds a lot easier. There were stories of kids like me, lost in the world and dealing with strange happenings. I would read for hours learning from adventures, analyzing worlds, and judging characters. I liked *Goosebumps* because it helped me be a kid in many ways. I was terrified and imagined all sorts of monsters and weird scenarios, but I was in the realm of make-believe. It was an escape from living a nightmare where no one really knew me, loved me, or checked in on me. My life was full of uncertainty and instability because I was moved once and knew it could happen again against my will. But the stories I read had a beginning, middle, and end. They were a pleasure to read when I feared my present without a clue as to how my story would end. In these books, there were happy endings, and each one of them contained love. The only love I knew was in the Dominican Republic, a place that was stripped from me and that I was not allowed to return to.

During middle school, I moved to Puerto Rico with my mother. Clara and Julio had left to live with her before me, and I caused hell to move there too. My stepmother was fed up and caved into the idea. My dad loved me very much, but I made it impossible for him to tolerate my late nights and nasty attitude. Sadly, after all my efforts to be with them, my time with my mother did not last long. I was not fond of the schools in Puerto Rico and told my mother that she should send me back to study in the United States if she wanted me to make it in life. There, I could play basketball because the school I went to did not have a team for girls, and I was the only girl on the boys' team.

Speaking Spanish 24/7 was also challenging. I never forgot how to speak, read, or write, but it was nowhere near an eighth-grade level. In school, I was yelled at by my Spanish literature teacher because I didn't know my last name was spelled with a tilde. I was so angry and appreciative at the same time. I knew it wasn't my fault, and I was thankful he helped me learn how to spell my name, but I also knew it was another reason kids called me "gringa." I was too Americanized. I was ultimately out of touch with my Dominican heritage and had no understanding of Puerto Rico either. I was so overwhelmed I even started to hate the weather. I hated the consistency of it. In Fajardo, I could not anticipate a change in the weather to spark some type of change in me.

Before I left Puerto Rico, I was grateful to have had a reunion with my grandmother. We went to D.R. on a ferry, which was not a pleasant experience for me. I was seasick the whole time and scared because I thought the boat was going to sink like the Titanic, and we were all going to drown. When I landed in Miches, my thought processing abilities were very disorganized. I had no clue how to communicate with my grandmother. I was not mature enough to verbalize the pain caused by the move.

My Spanish was not strong even though I had studied in Puerto Rico. And, for some odd reason, I even felt scared. It was so bizarre; I had wanted to see her, be with her, live with her, and there she was, but it was scary for me. She looked and smelled the same; smelling like comfort and warmth. In her eyes, I saw her excitement and disappointment at the same time. "Me cambiaron mi muchachita," was what I remember her saying. Little did she know how overwhelmed I was. All I could do was play basketball to distract myself and give people the cold shoulder. She knew me so well. She knew I was still that weird little girl, the bedwetter, la muchachita with the deepest fear of the dark. I don't remember much about my stay except a boy who pinned me down for a kiss at a birthday party. I was wearing a red tank top with flowers that had silver beads on them. I usually didn't dress very girly, but I liked the shirt and felt good wearing it. The kiss happened next to the birthday cake, and everyone was a witness. They all laughed it off, but it was uncomfortable for me.

My last move was with cousins in Lawrence, Massachusetts, and I grew a soft spot for the place. I flourished academically and in sports. I was a bit of a mess when I first started school. I had never seen so many brown people with curly hair in the U.S. New Haven was diverse, but Lawrence was full of primarily Dominicans; it is no wonder I felt a little bit at home. I enrolled at the Lawrence High School Campus and was placed in the Business Management and Finance High School (BMF).

At BMF, I met Julia, my Chilean gym teacher who became my second mom. I do not know where I would be without her. Most of the teachers who knew my backstory felt sorry for me. I had straight As but no parents to support me; they kept wondering how a sweet kid ended up with such bad luck. Good thing I was always in my world, stressing over schoolwork or playing basketball. Julia helped me out of my shell. She was the most animated gym teacher, and I loved her class, but I was also very uneasy. She had been in the school for a long time and would say, "OK, bye. I love you!" at the end of the most casual conversations with staff. I thought it was so cringy, and I always felt embarrassed. At sixteen years old, the words "I love you" were like saying He Who Must Not Be Named's name out loud. You only said that to your special people or spouse, and you never said it out loud for other people to hear. But Julia was different. Julia gave me an extra pair of uniform shirts and pants when she noticed my shirts would ride up my torso because I was growing tall and my pants were brincacharcos. Julia cheered me up every time I saw her and gave me different jobs setting up equipment for the class. In 2010, I applied to the College of the Holy Cross my senior year after visiting by chance with a friend and got accepted. Julia helped send me off to college with all the basics for my dorm. Thanks to her, I learned to say "I love you" and felt like I had someone in my corner.

Just when I started to settle into the crazy college workload, my grandmother died of bone cancer in late November. My oldest sister called me with my grandmother on the phone, so I could talk to her before she died. I had no money to afford a plane ticket, and I didn't know how to take a break from schoolwork. I did not talk to anyone about it. In my sophomore year, my family started adding me on Facebook, but I did not want to see any of them. I deleted that app immediately. It would be a couple of years before I got comfortable seeing them. I did not hate them; I just did not care about them.

Things took a major turn in my life a few weeks after my twenty-eighth birthday. After five summers of intense classes, I graduated with my master's degree, but the celebration was short-lived after I got a phone call that sent me back to Miches. This time, I returned under the worst circumstances. My oldest brother was murdered, and I returned for his funeral. I had not seen him since I last saw my grandmother. I had to deal with his traumatic death and face my past as an adult. I had to talk to people that watched me go so young and never reached out to ask how I was doing. They said my face never changed, that I had just gotten a lot taller. A part of me was angry at everyone, and a part was even madder at myself for holding on to something that happened so long ago. They only saw that I had made it financially and professionally and was an educated and responsible young woman. They did not know of the trauma I carried when I ached to be back to where I felt at home.

The saddest part about everything was that my brother and I did not even have a close relationship. He would text me a few times about getting my Netflix password, but I would ignore him. I didn't want to give him my login information because I had heard about my nephew, his youngest son. My nephew was abandoned as a baby at my grandmother's house by his mother. My brother didn't grow up with my mother, so I thought he knew better than to let his child grow up without a stable home. I kept hearing that my nephew was in a bad state. That he was out of control, a malcriado, and had been fighting with everyone. My mom asked me to adopt him when I was like twenty-three so that he could live with me in the US and have a chance at life. But I was just starting to put my life together; I couldn't even keep two thousand dollars in my savings account.

When I arrived at my grandmother's house, everyone was there grieving. I greeted my great-uncle, tíos, cousins, and people who looked vaguely familiar to whom Clara had to re-introduce me. When they asked if I remembered them, I said no. I wasn't going to lie, even though it would have made things less awkward. There was something that one of my cousins said that stayed with me throughout that evening. When we were on the side watching my mom argue with my uncle over the details of my brother's murder, she told me that she had been more of a sister to my brother than I ever was. It sounded harsh, but I wholeheartedly agreed with her. She did not know just how unstable my life had been. All she knew was that I had returned for my brother's funeral, a brother she knew I had not been there for when he needed me the most.

After the funeral, I stopped blaming my family for separating me from my grandmother. I matured and determined that I had to be the one to make amends with my past. I decided to look for jobs and make arrangements to move to the Dominican Republic. My oldest sister, who recently immigrated to the Bronx, grilled me about the decision. I was so mad at her for putting me in a position where I felt like I had to defend and rationalize my dream, but I understood her frustration. Most of my family thought it was reckless too, but I didn't care about their opinion. In the winter of 2022, I secured a job as a literature teacher at one of the top private schools on the island. I was ecstatic. I never got on the flight in August to start, though. Two months before takeoff, I was diagnosed with necrotizing myositis after going into the ER in Boston for difficulty swallowing and lifting my legs. In a matter of days, I lost my ability to walk, raise my arms and eat solid foods. I was bedridden. My diagnosis made me think about planning my funeral, which is why I have clung to my dream even harder. I am not dead yet, and I do not believe moving will be all I need to be whole, but it is a part of my story and journey to find all of my many pieces and lovingly put them back together.

La Leyenda del Vaporu/The Legend of Vaporub

Sinai Cota

I miss the minty oil rubs smeared between my mom's
fingers going up and down my back at night to soothe me.
After she was deported to Mexico, I'd dream of her healing hands
warm, trying to make me feel better as my airway struggled
to supply enough oxygen to my brain.
"Sana, sana." I'd hear her say, as the curtains of my eyes fell heavy
 "El Vaporu heals anything and everything mija."
It is the scent of my memories now that work
to heal me as an adult whenever I get sick.
I don't have her hands to massage me back into a safe slumber
or her voice to lullaby me with the prayer of *El Padre Nuestro*
She's miles away with a border that separates us.
But her love is medicinal transcending barriers.
I know now and always that her hot and cold minty
hands can be a jar away, next to my bedside, ready
to give me hope to start anew.

A Salt Eaters Litany

Nic Rodríguez Villafañe

Are you sure, sweetheart, that you want to be well?[1]
When you know a lot, it's harder to remember a lot
You already know the difficult shit
you just have to fall in love with it.

Are you sure, sweetheart, that you want to be well?
Physics tells us there are infinite parallel existences
Manifestation is just calling upon one of those times
Process blessings and shortcomings together

Are you sure, sweetheart, that you want to be well?
You have to apologize to the people you harmed
during your hurting, without expectations
you have to accept the way relationships change

Are you sure, sweetheart, that you want to be well?
When you choose your truth, there will always be loss
Nothing is more difficult than what you've been through
We're not that far yet, we're getting in position

Are you sure, sweetheart, that you want to be well?
Everybody don't deserve to be around you
You gotta defend your light with your life
Not everyone will be on the journey with you. That's okay.

Are you sure, sweetheart, that you want to be well?
Always trying to stay centered and balanced
can deny what you need to experience right now

Go feel.

---

1 Are you sure, sweetheart, that you want to be well? . . . . Just so's you're sure, sweetheart, and ready to be healed, cause wholeness is no trifling matter. A lot of weight when you're well." From Toni Cade Bambara's *The Salt Eaters* (1980).

Pyrite

Sofia Quintero

As soon as Gil and I lay down across the rug—side by side, head to toe—his pitbull, Cena says, "I'm going with you."

Gil lifts his head, his soft afro brushing against my bare ankle. "Yeah, Clara, let her go with you."

I look up at my professor as she stands above us, holding a large feather in one hand and an abalone shell cupping a bundle of burning sage in the other. "Can I take her?"

Professor Rivera laughs. "You couldn't stop her." She fans the smoke from the sage through the air above us. "Are you both comfortable?"

I reposition the pillow under my head until I smell the faint aroma of fabric softener steeped into the leg of Gil's camouflage pants. "Yeah," I lie. Gil says nothing.

"OK, you two. Close your eyes and take deep belly breaths. I'm going to start the music, and the process will begin."

"Yeah, Doc," says Gil. "'Cause my playlist is fire."

I slap my hand against his thigh. "Be serious!" Professor Rivera promised me that he would show up at her office tonight for this process. That he was in enough pain. But we've been best friends since grade school. Too long for me to not recognize that Gil's just humoring me by being here. Lo regaño yet I've missed this goofy side of him. Missed him.

"It's OK, Clara, now close your eyes." But I can't just yet because then this all becomes real. Professor Rivera shuts off the lights in her office and taps on the screen of Gil's smartphone. When I convinced him to let me do a soul retrieval—my first as a shaman in training—she sent him an email with instructions on how to prepare. No booze, no drugs, no TV or social media at least for twenty-four hours before the appointment. Wear comfortable clothes. Bring some kind of totem. A picture. A piece of jewelry. Something significant to him yet small enough for me to carry so Gil brings a piece of pyrite, which is in the front pocket of my jeans snuggled against my hip.

And most importantly, Professor Rivera asked Gil to send her a playlist of his favorite songs with only one condition. Unless they were chants or mantras, the songs could not contain any lyrics. Music that pulls Gil out of his head and into his body. When I warned her that the smartass would give her a bunch of hip-hop beats, Professor Rivera said that was actually perfect.

The last thing I see before I finally close my eyes is the aloe vera plant on the windowsill across Professor Rivera's office. I gave it to her for Christmas when she told me she wanted to incorporate more herbs and aromatics into her practice. Few people on campus know that when she's not teaching religion, the professor provides shamanic services. No one would blink an eye if she read tarot cards or cast natal charts. But ancestral healing and curse unraveling? She swears her protégés to secrecy. And I only became one because I vented to the oak tree by Carman Hall about a group project, and the tree told her.

I draw a breath deep into my belly like she had me practice daily for weeks as I wait for the first song on Gil's playlist. I imagine him, sitting on his fire escape thumbing through an app and stripping lyrics from the beats. As my breath slows and my head grows light, I try to guess the first sample from Gil's Top Ten. Definitely "Rebel Without a Pause." Wait. Maybe not. Gil loves the Dexter Wansel sample in "Money, Power, Respect," but that song's not appropriate for a spiritual ritual. Not that he cares about things like that.

Oh my God, Gil. If the Professor plays Gin and Juice, I'll kill you. Dead ass. I'll retrieve your lost soul and then I'ma kill you.

The keys of a piano trickle a storybook melody out of the Professor's speaker, and I grin. Of course, "Uptown Anthem." The beat drops, and Gil's foot begins to sway, grazing my hoop earrings. The song's perfect. Percussive. Repetitive. Hypnotic. I focus hard to train my attention to the beat and not the lyrics in my head. While I won't know where the soul retrieval will take me, I know that I'm not journeying to the spiritual realm to break, to bash, to roll or to smash. This version of the anthem agrees with me, the chorus chanting. *We gonna, we gonna, we gonna . . .*

The sample lures me into a trance until I feel Cena's warm and fuzzy tongue slide across my cheek. My eyelids creep open in time to see her dart across the room toward the window. I lift myself up on my elbows. Gil remains lying on the ground next to me in a deep sleep, but my professor is gone.

Cena says, "Clara, open the window!" She leaps onto the sill as I cross the room. As I open the window, I realize that the potted aloe vera plant is also gone. Outside a massive trunk of a birch tree stretches across the frame. I gaze upward, see the dingy sneakers hanging from one of the branches and realize this isn't just any tree. It's my favorite birch tree who lives in Starlight Park eight miles from Lehman College. All trees listen, but she is the first to respond to me.

"Madrina, what are you doing here?" I ask.

"To take you to the Upper World," she says. "Climb."

"Climb?" Madrina knows I'm afraid of heights. That's why I've never been able to pull off the raggedy tennies that hang from her lowest branch still thirty feet from the ground.

"No biggie," says Cena. She rears back then launches herself onto Madrina's trunk, scampering upward more feline than canine. Madrina laughs. "That tickles." Before disappearing into the clouds, Cena yells down at me, "Clara, come on!"

And although there are no crevices in Madrina's bark where I can plant my toes or dig my half-bitten nails, a pulse of energy emanating from her heartwood magnetizes me. I crawl up, up and up, like a superhero in a blockbuster movie. Still, I never look down.

When I reach the top, Cena is waiting, standing on the clouds as if they were pillows. "Just step onto that last cloud," she says. "It'll hold you, I promise."

I slowly rise to my feet and step gingerly on the cloud. With every step I take, the fog breaks open until it lifts away and a meadow of dewy grass stretches before me. Y esa maldita perra darts across the meadow like she's Toto in the poppy fields. I burst into a run. "Cena, hold up!"

She leads me to a lake where a lone rowboat lies on its side, half on land, half in the water. "He's on the other side. We have to take this across," Cena says. I shield my eyes from the sun and spot a forest about a mile or so away. I turn over the boat, finding the oars tucked underneath. While I push the boat into the water, Cena leaps into it. Then with the same care I stepped onto the cloud, I ease into it.

My last time in a rowboat was almost six years ago when I was twelve. My after-school program took us to Rock the Boat, an organization that gives people rides down the Bronx River while explaining the local ecology. Seven other girls and I followed the guide's instructions as we paddled north, our eyes peeled for beavers and eels. "Since you know how to climb trees, how 'bout you pick up an oar?" I say to Cena.

She holds up a white paw to flash the pink pads of her forelimb. "Do these look like hands to you?"

"Maldita perra."

I start to row, and the percussion of "Uptown Anthem" worms back into my skull. I pull the oars to the rhythm of the beat and wonder about Gil. Is he dreaming? Does he see us? If not us, what does he see? We come to an orange buoy with drippy black words spray-painted across it. I steer the boat close enough to read.

Lago de Recuerdos. The Lake of Memories. A chill creeps through my sweater, and I turn around. I can no longer see the shore we left. I look forward, and the woods ahead of us are gone, too. The waves beneath us start to swell, and my heart begins to race.

Cena senses my fear. "Keep going. We're almost there." She looks over the edge of the boat into the increasingly choppy waves. "And, Clara, you have to look in the water, too."

The surf rocks the boat. "No!" I say, clutching the oars, stabbing them into the lake. "No time. We have to get to the other side."

A wave crashes against the side, spilling a clump of moss into the boat, and I scream. As if to argue, another wave hits me on the opposite side and knocks an oar out of my hand. I scramble to retrieve it before the lake can swallow it. That's when I see our reflection in the water.

Gil and me. We're ten and traipsing along the Bronx River in Starlight Park. We're looking for rocks so he can teach me how to make them skip across the water. *The flatter, the better.* The glitter of a black stone catches the sunlight, and I pick it up. *Like this?* Gil takes it from me. *No, this is pyrite.* He offers it back to me. *You keep that.*

But I can tell he wants it. *You can have it* I say, handing it back to him. Gil smiles, tucking the pyrite in the front pocket of his hoodie before turning around and continuing along the riverbank.

I had forgotten that I was the one who found the stone and gave it to him when we first became friends.

Despite the choppy waters, I reach for our reflection, my fingers causing ripples. The image fades away, but as the waves propel the boat through the lake, I see Gil in each one. Leaning over an electronic keyboard at his uncle's music shop, Tonton Jean standing behind him, hand on Gil's shoulder. Standing up to that Dominican bully who finally moved away to the Heights. As we pass through the watery film of Gil's life, the pleasant memories lap gently against the boat while the troubled ones toss us about. The triggers become more frequent. I grasp the oars again and paddle like a hummingbird, flapping its wings only to hover in place. One of these waves depicts the reason a piece of Gil's soul left his body, but I just want to get us back to land as soon as possible.

"Clara, you have to look," says Cena. "Even if you're scared or it hurts. Especially if it hurts."

I paddle harder. Maldita pitbull! "Why?"

"Because healing requires witness. And it's how you'll know what to say when we find him to convince him to come back. You're safe, I promise you."

I draw the oars out of the water and pull them into the boat. Then finally I look over the side and into the waves. A primal urge deep in my gut surges throughout my body. It almost consumes me, driving me to dive into the waves and yank Lil Gil from his uncle's grip even if it means we could drown—anything to sooth the severe bite of Tonton Jean's betrayal, the salt of Lil Gil's shame. Then I relive the aftermath of Tonton Jean's passing—his death tearing off the tight lid over the trash that Gil had tamped down on his psyche. His powering down and abrasive distancing from those who know and love him most, preferring to medicate himself with forties and blunts in the company of strangers too occupied with their own suppression to ask questions. Then the realization sinks in that I cannot undo the harm done to him, and the urge in my belly morphs into a sickness that has nothing to do with the violent waves threatening to engulf the rowboat. A vile cocktail of rage and regret, heartbreak and hopelessness, it makes me gag, desperate to expel the trauma from my body. And just when I think it might end me—that drowning might bring peace—the waves subside and gently lap the rowboat to shore. "Why?" I wail. "Why did Gil suffer that? Why did I have to witness that?"

Cena climbs out of the boat and takes a few steps onto the marshy land, her paws leaving prints that immediately fade. She reads my mind and answers the questions. "Shame feeds the pain, and it thrives in the shadow. To bear witness—with love and without judgment—is to cast a light powerful enough to disintegrate its hold. And that's why I came with you; to do for you what you are doing for Gil."

"And what the fuck am I supposed to do with all this shit?"

"Let it go." Cena lays her head in my lap, and the warmth of her touch unleashes a well of sorrow. I sob so much, I threaten to capsize us on dry land. "Take all the time you need." Cena waits while I hallow myself until I become the very breath I need to muster to continue the journey.

I finally climb out of the rowboat and follow Cena into the woods. We trudge through bushes and vines until we come upon a river. It's the Bronx River. We're in Starlight Park. And down the bank I see Gil again at ten, skipping stones across the water. But he's not a full boy. Just a jagged shard of himself, occasionally reflecting the sunset. The piece of Gil's soul that fled to this realm so he could survive the trauma. I call his name. "Gil."

The sliver turns to me. "Clara?" His soul fragment glimmers like the pyrite I gave him.

His recognition, even though now I'm seventeen, cracks my heart open. "Si, mi amor," I say, remembering he's a child. "It's me. Please come here." And as this lost piece of Gil's soul runs to me, I can only see glimpses of his wholeness, flickering like a faulty light. But when Gil wraps his arms around my waist and presses his umber cheek against my chest, I feel the fullness of his life, our shared history.

He steps away from me, his face shimmering. "What are you doing here?"

"I came to bring you home."

Lil Gil's face falls. "I don't want to go home."

"Please," I say, "It's safe now. He's gone."

"Gone?"

"Yeah."

"Where'd he go?"

I have no answer yet realize I should not lie. "I don't know, Lil Gil, but what I do know is that he can't hurt you anymore."

Lil Gil sucks his teeth. "So what? If not him, somebody else. You trust people, and they fuck you over."

I'm at a loss for words because I can't tell him that's not true. I can validate his feelings and share my own experience. "After what you went through, I understand why you believe that and wish I could say that no one will ever hurt you again. What I can say is that there are so many people in your future who will know how to love you. They won't be perfect, but their love is worth it. You deserve to know them, and they you." I hesitate but add, "People like me."

The shard of Lil Gil shakes his head, growing opaque. He steps back as if to get out of my reach. Cena says, "Show him the rock."

I had forgotten about the pyrite. I dig into the front pocket of my jeans, scrape out the stone, and offer it to him. "Here. See?"

Lil Gil hesitates but then reaches for the pyrite. He holds it up to the sunlight, twisting it and smiling as it glitters. "You know what else they call this?"

"Yeah, I know."

"No, you don't," he teases.

"Fool's gold." Lil Gil concedes with a smile. "And yet you've kept it all these years."

"Yeah, well . . . it reminds me of you. And you're my best friend so . . . "

"Do you know what pyrite is good for?"

"What?"

"Protection."

Lil Gil twiddles the stone in his fingers. "Did you know that when you let me keep it?"

My heart almost burst to know that he remembers that moment like I do. "No. I didn't learn that until years later. That's why I brought it with me. And maybe . . . "

Lil Gil suddenly throws his arms around me again. I press my cheek against his forehead and hold him tightly. "Please come home. You're safe from him now. And I miss you so much." This is the part of Gil who jokes to make me laugh and not to mask his pain. The Gil who gets high on music and debates metaphysics with me at Starlight Park instead of downing forties with those dudes on the bleachers of Monroe HS. The one who can cherish the beauty in even the fool's gold.

"I miss you, too. I trust you." Lil Gil says as he buries his nose into my collar. "I'll go."

Cena leads us back through the woods towards the bank. The boat and oars sit where we left them. I gasp and point across the water. "Look!" Even though night is falling, the opposite land is visible. Cena hops into the boat, and Lil Gil and I shove it into the water before climbing into it ourselves.

A few minutes across the lake, Lil Gil leans over the side to drag his fingers into the water. "No, don't," I say, afraid that he'll see what I saw. That triggered by the memories that made him flee to this realm, Lil Gil will flee as soon as we make it to the opposite shore, and I'll lose him forever.

But when I reach for him, Cena blocks me. "It's OK now. On our way here, the waves reflect the waters of the past. On the way back, it holds glimpses of what's to come. His future holds peace."

"How do you know that?"

"Because the water is calm."

I stop rowing. Gil points at a roll of water glistening in the moonlight. "Is that me?"

Taking a deep breath, I pull in the oars and peek over the side. There in the wave is Gil now, napping on the rug in Professor Rivera's office, a tranquil smile nestled on his face. His image gives me courage to cast my eyes across the water searching for other visions of Gil's future. In one wave, he crosses the stage at Lehman College, decked in a Kelly green cap and gown to shake the dean's hand and accept his degree. When he steps off the stage, I'm waiting for him, dressed in yellow with tears in my eyes. When we hug, I cling to him.

Eager for more forecasts, my eyes bounce from wave to wave. In between two other drummers, Gil bangs on his boula as they play a rada. This is the drum of his dreams, and he has told me, and that they are very difficult to import from Haiti into the United States. My heart pounds with the joy of this witnessing of his dream come true.

Another wave reflects a still young Gil pacing the floor of a hospital room, cooing at an infant nestled in the crook of his arms. I look for me. For us.

And then I see the pier at the Marina del Rey overlooking the Long Island Sound. Gil wearing a tidy goatee and a tuxedo the color of steel, dancing a bachata with his bride. He steps back to whirl her around, and my heart sinks.

She's not me. I don't even know who she is. When I confronted Gil at the bleachers and begged him to let me try to help him, I had confessed my love for him. The next morning he texted me agreeing to the soul retrieval, and I took it to mean he loved me in the same way.

Something small and hard rips through the wave, rippling it across the surface of the lake. I turn around to look at Lil Gil. "Did you just throw something in water?"

He shrugs. "The rock."

I look to Cena who gives two pants. Her equivalent of a shrug. She explains, "Now that he's agreed to return, you don't need it anymore."

I snatch the oars and thrust them back in the water. As I paddle furiously across the river, Lil Gil stretches across the bottom of the boat and sleeps as if he has been awake for a thousand nights. By the time we reach the other side, my anger has given way to acceptance. Although time will tell if returning this piece of his soul to Gil will work—if he'll stop the smoking, the drinking, the recklessness—at least I tried to help him. Professor Rivera made it clear that to fulfill my purpose as a shaman, I have to take responsibility to replenish my empathy by attending to my own healing. Whether or not I succeeded in helping Gil, I convince myself that I have to love him from a distance and let him go.

A few feet from the riverbank, Cena dives into the water and kicks her way to land. I let Lil Gil sleep until I drag the boat to the shore. When I wake him up, he insists that I carry him so I unbutton my jacket and tuck the shard of him under my arm. I carry Lil Gil across the meadow and down Madrina's trunk, Cena trotting beside me the entire way.

I crawl through the professor's window. "Uptown Anthem" is still playing, and although I cannot see her, I feel Professor Rivera's presence. She says, "Kneel down next to him and blow the soul back into his body."

Cena jumps off the sill and onto the futon while I kneel down and crawl across the floor toward Gil. He snores. I unzip my jacket and pull out his soul fragment. Cradling it in my palms, I hover over Gil's chest. With a gentle breath, I blow on his soul and like the seeds of a dandelion, the whirl of his childish face wafts through the air and seeps into his heart. Then the music stops.

"You did it, Clara."

And that's when I sink to the rug, curl up against Gil and sob from exhaustion and regret.

My gasps for breath bring him out of the trance. He yawns, stretching his arms above his head. Then Gil notices me there lying beside him, crying. "Hey," he says as he rolls over and gathers me in his arms. "Hey."

"You should've told me," I cough. "Why didn't you tell me what he was doing to you?"

I wait a long time for an answer. "Because everyone loved him," Gil says. "*I* still loved him." He sits up, propping his elbows on his knees. Cena springs off the futon and onto him, pawing at his arms and licking his face. Gil nuzzles his face into her neck. Then he turns back to me, "What else did you see?"

I glance at Professor Rivera across the room, leaning against the windowsill beside the aloe vera plant. She folds her arms across her chest and presses her knuckles against her lips. The professor warned me that Gil will want to know what I discover, and that I have to use my discretion. That some of what I see is something the person needs to know. Other times they already know but perhaps have forgotten. And then there will be time when some of what I witness on my journey into the spiritual realm is best left there and to trust that the return of their lost soul is enough. I kept the depths of my feelings for Gil from the professor because I suspected she would insist on another protégé making the journey. Now I must wait until my next meeting with Professor Rivera to confess my bias and humbly ask her to counsel me through its steep cost.

I pull myself up, too. "You've got a lot of good things to look forward to, Gil." And in that moment, I make a new choice to stay in his future. Despite knowing he's going to break my heart, I still want to support Gil and witness his triumph. And not because my empathy needs to be repaid but because my love for him is worthwhile and true. "How do you feel?"

"I actually feel . . . " He searches for the word. " . . . lighter."

The professor says, "Good. That's good. You'll want to keep to yourself for a few days. Stay hydrated. Get lots of rest. And please no alcohol, no drugs. Not even weed." I expect him to crack a joke, but instead Gil just nods. "You might feel irritable, too, but that's just a sign of your soul reintegrating with your body. By week's end you'll feel much better than you have in a long time."

"And then what?"

"Whatever you need."

Cena says, "Tell 'em."

Gil cuts her a look. "Nosy ass pitbull."

"Tell us what?" I ask.

"My uncle. I see him. His ghost." Before I can gasp, Gil grabs my hand. "He's not hurting me or anything. He's just . . . there."

"Have you spoken to him?" asks Professor Rivera. Gil shakes his head. "OK, once you're up to it, ask your uncle what he wants." As part of my training, she taught me that our ancestors need four things from us—acknowledgment, validation, understanding, and forgiveness. My intuition tells me that what Tonton Jean needs most from Gil is his forgiveness.

It surprises me when Gil doesn't rocket to his feet, cursing under his breath and grabbing for Cena's leash, to run out the door. Nor does he fire a barrage of questions or objections at my professor. Gil just nods as he strokes Cena's back. This tells me that maybe the healing is working. That I actually helped him.

He stands up and reaches for Cena's leash where he hung it behind the office door. From where I still sit on the rug, I look up at him. "OK if we go home together?"

Gil shrugs. "Sure. I mean, we live in the same complex." Not the answer I wanted, but I accept it. But he does hand me Cena's leash so he can shake the professor's hand, and he doesn't request that I give it back.

We leave the building and start across the campus. Once we reach the boulevard, he asks me questions. Not about his soul retrieval but about shaman training. I answer as best as I can, but I keep to myself that soon enough he will know firsthand because this is the destiny we do share. This is also why Professor Rivera knew Gil was ready to heal. His role in our tribe is to play the drum and serenade the resistance to sleep.

When we enter the subway station, I open my crossbody bag and fish for my wallet. In the pocket where I keep it, I feel a lump. Pyrite. I chuckle and offer it to Gil who is waiting for me by the turnstile.

He looks at it and smiles. Taking Cena's leash instead, Gil says, "Nah, you keep that." Then he taps his debit card twice against the scanner, paying for both our rides.

As I walk through the turnstile, I realize that no matter what life brings, Gil will always be my best friend. Now that he knows that I will not turn away from his pain, he will hold space for mine. Together we will heal ourselves and others, expanding our tribe.

I close my hand around the pyrite, and Gil and I continue our journey home.

La Luz

Kate Foster

Aveces,

pienso que la luz más hermosa se puede encontrar
entre medio de las olas y no por el reflejo del sol

si no por los secretos que guarda
por lo que nos dice y también lo que se callá

veo como la arena entre mis dedos
desvanece cada grano una lágrima llorada

Aveces,

lo más radical es simplemente existir
existir entre ola y arena

existir entre el secreto y la verdad
existir entre lo oscuro y la luz

Existir
Existir
Existir

JUSTICE
DEFIANT WORLDMAKING

A Recommendation

Edyka Chilomé

For you reading this

painfully recognizing the season

consider setting aside diversion

and being brave enough to see

you are a seed in potent darkness

reach for the cool water

find pleasure in thundering night

touch the earth that is your skin

call in the magic buried in your blood

dare to break open in climax by your own hands

for our work now is to bloom beautiful in chaos

and return home come winter

Mariposa

Marcela Rodriguez-Campo

I am learning to
hold hands with
my inner three-year-old.
To coax her out
of the basement
I have hidden her,
tenderly ask her to show me
where the monsters live.
I want to walk next to her,
watch the spring in her
resilient curls bounce,
listen to her laugh again.
Explore the dark places
that I have kept from myself,
memorize the number of steps
between each light switch
with eyes wide open and see all of it.
I want to honor all the fears
that kept her fists clenched,
and then soften her stoic jaw.
Help her release all
that she has hoarded.
I want to set her free,
release her,
let her be a kid again.
For far too long,
I have kept her
pinned between
scapula and rib.
I thought I was protecting her,
but butterflies will injure
their wings to escape.
All fear, no fairytale.

That little girl

is pure artwork.
A heartbreaking display
of innocence.
Here sits, the only proof
that she ever lived.
In writing her
I set her free,
I return her wings.

Fierce Gorditx Coming Home

Dafne Faviola Luna

I, Dafne Faviola Luna, am Fat. Not chubby, curvy, gordita, chunky, plus size, or big-boned, but capital-F Fat! My fatness does not hide, nor can it be hidden because it's an excess of me. It is in your face when you look at me, leer at me, stare at me, and judge me. It rubs against you when I sit next to you, walk by you, or more like squeeze by. It yells at you when you talk with me, at me, and for me. I am seriously fat. I do not mean fat as in ugly, motherly, gluttonous, dumb, uneducated, or diseased. I mean fat as an adjective relating to the excess of my body.

Being fat, brown, and queer in Amerikkkan society means I've had the "pleasure" of being inundated with information about what good bodies are. In magazines, television, movies, commercials, and across all social media platforms I see thin light-skinned and light-eyed women who are revered: Britney Spears, Jennifer Aniston, and Scarlett Johansson. As a queer person, many of our cultural icons are similarly built, such as Ellen DeGeneres, Cher, and Lady Gaga. In my personal life I also get told what good bodies are. When friends and family comment on someone's weight loss and applaud them for it because they look so pretty now; or when the one Tía who I never see asks me what I plan to do about my problem. According to society, fat bodies are not good bodies. Ideologies and expectations of what my body is and isn't comes from doctors, teachers, family members, friends, and everyone and anyone.

My first memory of shame is at around the age of seven. I remember sitting to the left of my mom in an uncomfortable brown faux leather seat with metal arms. We were both facing an ugly evergreen metal desk that I kept kicking with my feet. Behind the desk I remember a woman with dyed blonde hair with a short teased out wave style. I do not remember what my mom and her talked about, but I remember the word *pesada* y *muy gordita*. Now mind you, by then everyone called me *Gordis* or *Gorda*, but it was not until that initial appointment that I began associating *Gorda* with something bad. After that the diets did not stop until I left home.

While the dietician visit was the first moment of shame for me, being femme, queer, and Chicana placed me in too many "unfortunate" situations that created more moments of self-hate. Moments such as being sexually harassed from a young age by older Latino and White men, being told to not talk about my queer relationships with family, and a stranger on a bus saying a fat girl shouldn't wear skirts. The various attacks on my body, instigated by pathologized sizeism, patriarchal toxicity, xenophobia, and queerphobia facilitated my extreme dissociation to the extent that even now I still struggle to talk about my body and myself as one whole being. Even though I've been in therapy for many years I do not look at myself in the mirror often which creates this feeling of not having a body but being hyperaware of my body at all times. I can feel the jiggle and rubbing of my body at different touch points but can completely ignore that it exists. I internalized the hateful and violent experiences inflicted onto my body to such an extent that it has been easy for me to ignore the pain, resist the hunger and thirst, and deprive myself of pleasure because I was protecting myself, but not my body.

My declaration of "Fierce Gorditx Coming Home" is a shout-out to our Joteria's ability to make any space or place with other queers a home-space, familia. What I am trying to say is that for me my queerness is my home base. My "othered" sexuality and my difference from the very heteronormative, cis-normative, and male-centered upbringing pushed me out, meaning I had to root myself in my queerness. Therefore, it only made sense that my fatness would also find home there. I wholeheartedly believe that if I were straight, I would have conformed to being a wife to a man and having kids. I would have never run away from that reality. My queerness saved me from that life, and I was forced to find an escape in it. Having an othered body, a fat one, one that is allegedly so different from the norm implies my fatness is also queer. While I cannot say that my fat femme body is nurtured by the mainstream White gay and lesbian communities, I can say that my identity as a Chicana feminist and fat femme allowed me to find communities that held my body in tenderness and empowerment. In this community I found fellow fats, queers, and femmes such as artist Laura Aguilar, LeighAnna Hidalgo, and

Caleb Luna. I attended body positive events and had someone encourage me to wear a crop top. These moments made such an impact to my inner fat kid who was constantly told to hide and disappear.

My sexuality has been a place and space of resistance to the heteronormative standards of my upbringing. Therefore, as a lifestyle of resistance my queerness has been front and center in everything I do, from my career choices, locations I live in, relationships I make, and my popular media consumption. I can confidently say I am very, very queer. However, in my journey to body acceptance and healing I realized that I do not approach my body with the same fervor and passion, or even tenderness, as I do my sexuality.

But if my fatness is queer, then why haven't I approached my body through my queerness? In all honesty, it's been fear. Fear of seeing the shapes of my body. Fear of touching my body and not liking it. Fear of realizing I actually hate myself and not because society made me do that. Thinking about the wondrous, beautiful, and powerful feelings that I do associate with queerness I am starting to think that I don't really have to fear hating myself any more than I already have.

Coming out as queer was life changing for me. So here and now I am coming out as Fat. I am Fat and this is me. I am a queer Fat Chicana femme and I reject society's need to hate myself. I can queerly love my queer body. I can make a stance against fat oppression, the same way I tackle queerphobia and transphobia. I will tell everyone and come out constantly about my fatness because every single time I say it, it gets easier. Maybe, just maybe, being Fat is like being Queer. It might mean being in community with other fatties, eating food, touching our shapes, living authentically, and enjoying our life as carefree people. So I will bring my fat body home to my BIPOC queer community because I need a safe space to land. I need a safe space to heal and a community that has my back, the way it has for my queerness. So, to other fat queers out there I have your back too.

Time Travel

Hector Luis Rivera

Time traveling,
unraveling each second,
each moment I'm testing duality
by manifesting, light, liberty,
I'm taking flight,
sonic boom Boricua bright
that shines into the night

to be the son of the Sun
is like one with the One,
an apprentice of the drum
made from barrels full of rum,
child of the sugarcane
like blood in Ponce runs,
fertilizing resistance
like freedom is won,
I'm a starchild, voodoo child,
that's where I'm from,
righteous ready rhythms
rocking rare rican puns,
reflections upon inspection
directions ain't done,
on this planet for a second
my thoughts weigh a ton

time traveling,
unraveling each second,
each moment I'm testing duality by manifesting,
light, liberty,
I'm taking flight,
sonic boom Boricua bright
that shines into the night

wind is connected to change
like chains to our brains

rich port, blood sport, pass the quart,
aimed to rearrange,
our DNA, but Oya don't play,
water, candle, rum, drums, and pray,
hear the thunder, ride the rays,
pidele piquete, the primo pays,
it's alchemy, energy,
air, fire, water, earth magically,
making moves monumental,
planting seeds,
Albizu in Lares,
freedom's tree,
rooted resilience,
see my steez,
beacon of brilliance,
divine decree,
rican resistance,
liberty,
leaving lyrical lessons
'till we all free

time traveling,
unraveling each second,
each moment I'm testing duality by manifesting,
light, liberty,
I'm taking flight,
sonic boom Boricua bright
that shines into the night

"Do you see me?": Musings on the Pain of Anti-Blackness or Black Denial/Rejection in Latinx Spaces

Biany Pérez

"Where are you from? No, really?! Dominican?! You can't be."—Anonymous person interrupts my phone conversation with my Spanish speaking mami while riding the city bus.

"Ella bonita pero muy negra. She is pretty but too Black."—Two darker-skinned cisgender men sitting across from me on the NYC subway talking about me in Spanish.

"Soy Dominicana. Tu hablas español muy bueno para ser Negra. Si, porque soy Dominicana. No, tu no puedes ser Dominicana?!"—Bodega Chats with strangers

"It is not our differences that divide us. It is our inability to recognize, accept and celebrate those differences."—Audre Lorde, *Sister Outsider: Essays and Speeches*

I discovered my creative and queer Black/Afro-Caribbean feminist ancestor Audre Lorde in college. It was at the same time that I developed a radical Black feminist consciousness. Audre Lorde gave me a voice and an understanding as to the importance of holding, embracing, and celebrating across differences. This striving towards difference is one way we honor the full spectrum of one's humanity and experiences. It allows us to hold on to the many ways folks show up as themselves. It is in the recognition that we are able to experience who we are as a collective. Through recognition, we create spaces where differences are welcome, where discomfort is an invitation to learn and grow, and where we can unlearn old narratives that keep us collectively stuck in a painful past caused by oppression, colonialism, supremacy, and trauma. We get to be in right relationship with others as well as ourselves.

Recognition allows us the space to say I see you; I honor and make room for all parts of you. The absence of this often leads many to be in the constant stubborn striving for sameness that makes our uniqueness, our histories, our experiences, our gifts, talents and perspectives invisible. I wish for the moment that Latinx spaces can celebrate and embrace the differences that I/ we carry as Black/Afro-Indigenous Latinx folks.

It was not easy to muster up the courage to write these words. To share my stories and experiences with an issue/concern that I've often held close to my heart because in my community, the Latinx community, racism is the dirty secret that so many want to keep hidden from the light of our collective and individual awareness. My experiences with anti-Black racism often left me feeling alone and invisible. This invisibility often served a dual purpose: *to keep me silent, hidden and in the shadows and also led me to carry the pain and weight of the projections from those who denied my existence.* There is a silencing that happens when you attempt to discuss racism within our communities. It is like airing out dirty laundry when all you want to do is keep it hidden from our collective view. It is a stain of shame that we continue to carry, and we often don't expose its destructive tendencies. Shame tends to live and thrive in silence. This has become a wound that we carry without acknowledging the harm that it causes each of us in Latinx communities. The denial and outright disavowal of the many shades of Black, African, and Indigenous that are a part of the Latinx diaspora is a wound that remains raw, unmetabolized, and not yet ready to become a scar. The wound runs so deep that the persistent denial sustains the contagious wound making it impossible for the medicine of truth to bring forth healing.

Fellow social worker and shame researcher, Brené Brown, contends most fervently that vulnerability is the birthplace of courage, compassion, and connection. I am emboldened by the power of vulnerability. In writing this essay, I am meeting the space where vulnerability lies, it lives in the liminal space between courage and fear. The fear of being fully seen. The courage to be fully seen. Vulnerability holds the truth of my diverse identities. Vulnerability is the spark that lights my way. The fear of being seen, embraced, and listened to. This fear turns into anger, into ancestral rage. My ancestors and those who came before me had to deal with the fear of not being truly seen. Their rage is my rage. Their courage is my courage. I use my voice to honor their voice. I fight to be heard. I speak my truth unapologetically. Both fear and courage offer me the space of recognition. There is a fear that I am exposing some unthinkable and scary truths about my community. The truth must be brought to light. The courage to speak these unspeakable truths so that those that come after me don't carry the weight, don't carry the pain of not being seen by folks who are supposed to be our people. It is time for me to unburden myself from the weight of this pain.

I am the insider, outsider of a community that continues to attempt to deny my existence. Most times I feel like an outsider because anti-Blackness keeps me at a distance, keeps me othered from other Latinx folks who question my identity. Anti-Blackness pushes me to the margins in an already marginalized space. Anti-Blackness activates the parts of me that already feel exiled inside. It activates my tender parts by making me feel like I am not good enough, not smart enough, and most importantly not Latinx enough. My brown skin. My kinky curly hair. My big nose and lips. The way I talk. The fact that my Spanish accent is no longer recognizable. All these parts of me get placed in the limelight to be dissected and dismissed. The presence of my African ancestors keeps some Latinx folks away. They see me and they deny me. They deny me, they deny themselves.

"You can't be my son. Your skin is as dark as the bottom of this cooking pot."—Potential Paternal Grandfather who rejected my papi.

I imagine my father, who walked out on us when I was six years old. I imagine he didn't think he was capable of parenting us the way he wasn't parented. His trauma became my trauma. I imagine my father, his pre-teen self, drumming up the courage to walk to that affluent neighborhood in Santo Domingo to meet his biological father. He nervously and excitedly prepares to meet the father who didn't raise him but who's present absence colored his life. From what he shared with me, my father felt like such an outsider growing up. I guess he was hoping for some semblance of belonging. He was hoping that in daring to meet this part of his identity he would feel less alone in the world.

Papi was fortunate to be raised by fierce Black Dominican womxn. These beautifully dark chocolate reinas loved my father but I guess for him it wasn't enough. Poverty made it hard for him to feel the love. He had to drop out of school as a pre-teen so that he could help provide for the large family he was born into. The Pérez matriarchs who were fiercely independent and resilient never made my father feel less than, but the world wasn't as kind to him.

My father, his teenage self, drums up the courage to knock on the door. Drums up the courage to meet the man who is his father. Only to be rejected and denied. "Tu no puede ser mi hijo. Mira, tu eres muy negro." "You can't be my son?! You are too Black!" His father points to the bottom of the burned and gently used dutch pot. Those steel pots used for making arroz con frijoles, where you burn it just long enough that the Concon is just right! Yeah, that perfect steel pot with a charcoal colored burned bottom, my papi didn't pass the test. He couldn't be the son of this light-skinned, he "think he white-skinned man."

Belonging is our birthright but what happens when we don't feel like we belong in spaces and communities where we call the same place home. Like my father, who has felt denied, rejected and abandoned merely for the melanin in his skin.

> When i reflect upon the theme of this anthology: Latinx pain
> i think about invisibility
> Being othered
> being pushed to the margins in marginal spaces,
> Cast aside
> Denied
> Dismissed
> Silenced in spaces that are already at the edges.
> Questions that activate me, the ones that bring aches in my bones
> Where are you from?
> What are you?
> Really?
> They pierce my soul, make my blood boil, like whiplash, like a slap
> in the face
> Because I know that these questions are already laced with judgment,
> laced with answers that project upon me as if i am
> this blank slate or deadless object.
> When they ask they already craft a response
> they are looking for their answer,
> they're not listening to mine.
> So when someone asks me what are you, where are you from
> The question brings with it assumptions
> the question is tainted with judgment and latinx denial
> when i say i'm latinx, resistance, othering, fear, doubt,

*it's a reminder that i really don't belong in latinx spaces even tho
i know i do,
sometimes i wish that question was not asked.
Sometimes i wish they would just listen to me, to my story, to my
words.
Why can't they see me?
Why can't they see me in them?
Because i remind them of their denial
Because i remind them of what they could be
I remind them of their potential they are scared of
I remind them of the history they long to deny
They deny me, they deny themselves
They dismiss me, they dismiss themselves
They reject my blackness, they reject their own blackness*

*We carry the pain of our past
We carry the stories of our ancestors
We inherited the racial wounds of latinx denial
But we also carry the hope of our future
We unearth these shameful truths
We lessen its power over us*

*Latinx pain is the pain of Black denial
The pain of not being seen, heard or understood.
This pain is transmuted, transformed
This pain of being Latinx
Becomes something else
My truth reveals the beauty of my differences
My truth reveals the gift of recognition*

*Justice work is knowing ourselves
Justice work is embracing our differences
Justice work is embodying difficult truths
Justice work is healing work
Justice work is truth telling
Justice is calling the truth in
Justice is centering Blackness in Latinx spaces
Justice is sitting with what has been hidden for too long*

*I am not going anywhere
We ain't going 'no where.
Blackness is here to stay.
Black Latinx folks have been here.
And we ain't going 'no where*

ode to the upside-down flag stamp on every letter i mail

Gabriella Navas

you are yet another habit i have inherited from my papi:
the man who taught me that an upside-down american flag
is a sign of distress, who pledges allegiance only to the
flag of lares. i had a dream the other night where we all
took to the streets: stormed our old middle school classrooms
after hours, scaled flagpoles to turn the flags on their heads.
but in the morning, i woke up and all the flags were still right-
side up and half of america refused to acknowledge our grief.
look, i know that this is purely symbolic, and i know that i am
not changing the world by turning you upside-down, but
at the very least, you are how i signal to the people i love
that i see them, and their distress, and that i am on my way.

Ode to Amara La Negra,

after Melania-Luisa Marte

Lysz Flo

"Ode to always fighting to be seen despite the erasure"

When they say Latina,
      I wonder if they include me?
      in their mental picture vs Univision.
Or is it a person who looks like they speak Spanish?
With this unspoken assumption,
I remain never to be counted as one either
Even when Mami says, "ella es mi hija, ella habla en español."

Ode to all the reggaeton videos
 that don't have girls that look like me
                 I dance anyway
as if looking more like our colonizer
would make me more delectable
as if all of these blood-filled words
don't gain me access into places I don't quite belong
             I walk in anyway, smiling at their bewilderment
eating my *Rrrrs* and talking my kreyol
singing Bad Bunny while loving Don Omar
because he was one of the few negritos,
I could truly love.

Speak with my acento,
like this tongue don't miss my way around
Taino existence before Cristobal Colón
by the way *get maman* ese cabrón

The rest of the world thinks resembling
robbers, thieves, and asesinos
makes me a beacon.

Ode to the mejórando la rasa mentality

and Mami marrying a Haitian man did just that.

Don't I look so Afro,
so like mi Madre,
so skin tone Papi,

Ode to every grito of wepaaaa,
autocorrect finally recognizes,
sway of my hips
intuitive dance to El Gran Combo,
ode to the Kompa,
I dance in the living room
hoping Papi's espiritu joins in from time to time.

"Ode to the AFRO being first before Latina."

A symbol of freedom runs
through these Haitian Puerto Rican veins.
Ode to this diaspora of hidden Black roots
who take up space con tumbao y la Bemba colora.

Altagracia

Amaris Castillo

A grinning Altagracia looks back at me, yet again, as we climb the last flight of stairs. The woman who birthed me didn't say much on the ride from the airport. Only frequent glances at me through starry eyes, as if still unsure I am really here, in New York, with her.

I force a smile back.

We reach the landing and make a sharp right before stopping in front of door 3A. Altagracia digs into her large Louis Vuitton purse for the key to her apartment. The metal door screeches open to a long, narrow hallway. Altagracia is quick, grabbing both my maletas to pull them to their destination. I follow the click-clack of her heels and take in this place for the first time. Disappointment lays in wait as I peer at the hallway walls. I'm looking for any photographic signs of me.

The apartment tour is not really a tour. Altagracia barely acknowledges her cramped kitchen and we quickly pass a sala with oversized furniture. There is her room to our right and, at the very end, another. Altagracia opens the second bedroom door and waves me inside. It is small, but tidy. In the left corner is a bed, neatly made with two pillows and a half dozen stuffed animals. The sole window stretches up to the ceiling.

My new room is bigger than the one I shared with my abuela back home, something I would have been happy about under a different circumstance.

"I bought you some clothes." Altagracia's voice—etched in worry—cuts through our silence. She can't seem to mask the pathetic hope I know she holds for our relationship. She makes a joke about how the cold is unforgiving here, how we aren't in Santo Domingo anymore.

"Your favorite color is red, right?"

Her heels click quickly to an open closet at the far left of the room. In it is a monochromatic blur of tops in different shades of red, and a handful of sweaters and a puffy winter coat. On the shelf above, just below a hanging light bulb, are some folded pants—also red—and a maroon-colored wool hat adorned with a bright red pompom.

"Actually, it's yellow now." My back is turned to her.

"No te preocupes," she chirps. "I saved the receipts and can return them at the store. Yellow is very pretty."

Altagracia pushes the maletas into a corner while I study the rest of the room. There is a wooden dresser with a small television on top and beside it a hairbrush and some hair accessories. There is a desk with a stack of new notebooks and an empty Café Bustelo jar filled with pencils and highlighters—surely a signal that she wants me to enroll in the local community college. At seventeen, I know I need to do something with my life but haven't decided what that is yet.

The woman who birthed and later abandoned me then walks over to the window and draws the curtain, filling the room with a slice of bright August afternoon. This is to become my new home. She turns to look back at me, pride wrinkling her 40-something-year-old face. She wants me to love this place as much as she does. Perhaps more than that, though, she wants to feel love.

"There's life here, too," she says. "You will grow into it. I know this." Without another word, Altagracia leaves the room, closing my new door quietly behind her.

I walk over to the window, the bottom half of which has an iron guard. It is plain, not like the ones with flair and curls at the ends like in the Dominican Republic. My hands grip onto the bars. I ask myself if this is how it will always be between my mother and I. This uneasiness and so many words unsaid, knitted into something neither her nor I can digest. Those years in New York, away from me—how did this woman fill her time?

I close my eyes and will them back to the existence I was comfortably in just hours ago, with my Abuela Romana. In the sala, savoring my last café with her. Trying not to record her face into my most cemented memory, but unable to help myself. Every time I looked over at her, I found my abuela staring right back at me, her own eyes shining with a hint of tears.

***

Back in Moca, there was this game my mother and I liked to play. It began years ago, when I already knew how to count. On days when the clouds sagged, Altagracia would invite me to sit on the tile floor with her in the two-bedroom house we shared with my abuela, and together we'd inhale the cleansed air. We'd take turns counting the motoconchos that flew by, imagining where they were headed. It was fun to make up things we knew nothing about.

Altagracia was stunning, her skin a rich caramel and her hair always kept in a low, tidy ponytail. She had a dark mole on her chin, which she always pretended to remove to give to me whenever I asked why I didn't have one like hers. My mole was on my right shoulder. So there we would be for more than an hour, counting motoconchos and pretending to exchange beauty marks.

When I was thirteen years old, Altagracia sat me down one evening to tell me she was planning on heading to New York City in search of work. In our town of Moca, parents leaving first to carve a future in Nueba Yol was not uncommon. And so the children would stay behind to be raised by someone else until it's time to send for them. A tía, los abuelos, hasta una vecina. I was blessed, though, because my mother left me with my Abuela Ramona, who loved me fiercely.

On the first night after my mother left, I sat on the floor and placed my weight against the open entryway of our house. Heavy rains weighed on our corner of Moca that night, and I felt her absence with each pelt hitting our roof of corrugated tin. On rainy days my mother always liked to open the door, ignoring Abuela Ramona's warnings about getting sick.

But that first night without Altagracia, my abuela called for me to get up from the floor. In our sala was a giant mecedora with a cotton chair pad that years of wear flattened into nothingness. My grandmother bid me to sit there with her. She engulfed me in her thick arms.

We had nothing to say, really. My spider legs spilled to the floor as she began to rock us both. My cries grew louder until my chest began heaving. Her large palms patted my back until there were no more tears left.

The next morning, we were awoken by a phone call from my mother. She told me she'd arrived safely and that she had an interview later that week for a factory job. I swallowed the tiny knot of disbelief in my throat that she had made the decision to leave her only child for the unknown. I wished her well. This knot—what felt like a rock—would bob up every time someone in my barrio asked about "my Mami," as if I was still an extension of her. As if I spoke with her all the time.

Months passed and the only physical connection I had with my mother were the larger-than-life cardboard boxes she'd ship to us filled with clothes, shoes, soaps and other items that I swore could also be found here in Moca. I would run my fingers over each item, knowing she had placed each in the box herself. Sometimes I smelled the clothes to see if I could detect her vanilla scent.

The phone calls Altagracia would make to us twice a day—in the early morning and just before bed—gradually became one nightly call. She promised she would bring me to be with her in New York as soon as she was able. She sent us money regularly, more on our birthdays. When she picked up a second job as a waitress, our phone began ringing every other day. I refused to take the initiative and call her myself.

It took me some time to realize my mother wasn't coming back to me. By the six-month mark of her absence, I stopped sitting by the doorway whenever it rained. And as each year passed, even though she visited when she could, my heart grew a harder shell still.

***

I'm in my new bed in Brooklyn now. If I close my eyes tight enough, I can picture my Abuela Ramona's gap-toothed smile, her skin the color of dulce de leche, her gray eyebrows as thick and lovely as they were in the few photos she had from her youth. Even though she didn't want to come to Nueba Yol, my abuela is with me, always. I pull out her photo from my wallet and study her face.

My head begins to throb. I need sleep. How drastically my life has changed in a matter of hours. Now I'm in a place with a strange, metal tongue. The buildings here look the same—aged brown brick. Brooklyn's noise is different from Moca's noise. Here there are fire alarms, car honks, yells in English. Un ambiente distincto.

I am awakened later by the sound of floor creaking. That's when I see her standing a few feet from me. "Oh, you were sleeping," Altagracia says, almost nervously. "I am sorry. I didn't mean to frighten you."

She stares at me. Her dark eyebrows knit together and she takes in a breath. There is emotion behind Altagracia's face, but I can't quite place it. I stare back at her, afraid to blink and miss this moment.

"I'm sorry about your favorite color," she says. "I know I have lost track of the things you enjoy and—"

"You've lost track of so much," I interject. Her mouth gapes open. My body warms up as anger settles in.

"Now you want to be a mother and bring me here and shove clothes and money and the promise of a new beginning in my face."

I shock even myself, but the feeling is gone as quickly as it comes. I want every word to cut into her. I tell her about waiting over a year to see her and spending a total of four years in Moca when I most needed her. Told her that a daughter needs her mother.

Her body is still. I hope every word cuts into her over and over again. I need her to say sorry. Not wanting to see her reaction, I turn back to the window. On the sidewalk below, people go about their daily lives. The hissing of a bus braking to pick up passengers fills the silence. I hear the floor beneath Altagracia's feet creak as she places something by the edge of my bed. She leaves again. When I turn my head, I notice a photograph there. It's one I had never seen before, of me and her sitting near our old door —admiring the rain.

I come from dreams

Ana Miramontes

So big they had to expand in two countries.
So big that picturing them, at some point, didn't make sense.
So big that two languages were not enough.
I come from dreams of the altars at school for
"Dia de Muertos." From wanting to eat the fruit,
but being afraid to eat the ghost.
I come from dreams of waking up in the middle of the night,
looking at the moon and realizing what true happiness is.
Dreams that made me wake up and grab a pen and paper, so
I could remember. Dreams that remind me that I belong in
many places. I come from dreams that dictate my reality, and
from realities that have been created in my dreams. I come
from dreams of eating my dad's tortillas, my moms frijoles,
and my brother's candy.
I come from colors warm as the soil that holds mi casa, from
cacti that my mama puts in my breakfast, from a pride that
protects me just as much as my rosary, from a family that will
never let me grow up, nor ever leave me alone.
I come from my pa, my mami, my tita, and my abuelita. I come
from what I have created of myself, from what I've been taught
from my gramma's prayers.
I come from defending every word I say,
overthinking it, regretting it,
remembering that dad didn't teach me to retract. From "Mejor
cabrona que pendeja."
I come from them, they are my dreams,
my realities.

Revolutionary Dreams, Fevered Pursuits

David Luis Glisch-Sánchez

Most people have come to believe that Cuba is a word, a name that denotes a place—the largest island in what is now known as the Caribbean/el Caribe. As a child, I learned early on, that Cuba was less a place, and more of an idea. An idea, I often fear, that teeters on the verge of collapse, struggling to uphold the weight of the meanings people and communities—both on and off the island—have placed in these four little letters. Cuba is a vessel that holds dreams and nightmares, hope and despair, possibility and decay, revolution and repression. Within this maelstrom of meaning and crucible of contradictions, I have struggled as a child of a cubana refugee and a member of the Cubanx diaspora to forge my own understanding and relationship to this idea. The ideas we hold about "Cuba" are important because what we come to think and believe about this place is ultimately what we come to feel, think, and believe about the people who call this place home.

Paradise was my first idea of Cuba. The smells, sounds, and stories of mi familia were my port of entry to this paradise. The aromatic notes of un sofrito, the syncopating rhythm of Celia Cruz and other guaracheras, and the volume and liveliness with which cuentos were retold gave me glimpses into the land my family left. As a young child, I struggled to understand why my mother and her family left this seeming paradise. It had to be a mistake. I should have been born there; we should be living there. Certainly, my family wouldn't willingly forego life in La Habana for an existence in Milwaukee, WI; or would they? My young mind searched for more ideas to help me understand what I felt had to be a grave error. I wanted and needed to understand the absence and void I sensed in my body.

Revolution was my second idea of Cuba. As a child, I thought revolution was a big word, literally and conceptually. From how mis tías y tíos spoke of la revolución it quickly became clear that it was not a good thing. This confused me. In school, we learned of the American Revolution, and other independence movements throughout the Americas, and they were not talked about as a bad thing; so why was Cuba's revolution any different? I am not insinuating that the American Revolution or any colonial nation-building project is good; rather I am pointing out that certain revolutions are deemed acceptable while others are not, and that the dividing line is often around capitalism and whiteness. I have come to understand that people's feelings and opinions about Cuba and revolution are infinitely complex; tangled in a web of historical struggles, class and racial conflicts, personal loss, and collective grief. It would be years before I could even begin articulating this understanding.

According to most members of my family, Cuba was perfect. Better than any other place on Earth, that is until Fidel Castro and his revolution changed all of that. But this explanation never felt accurate to me. Possibly, this was because my mother was the outlier in our family. She explained to mi hermana and I that although la revolución established a deeply repressive and antidemocratic regime, life in Cuba beforehand was hard and corrupt for many. This made sense. Real revolutions cannot be started or maintained unless there is widely held and felt frustration and resentment with how things are. I have always been grateful to my mother for this insight and knowledge. At the time, I did not understand, but now I do, that she was showing me/us how we can liberate ourselves from the binary thinking that often has a stranglehold on our ideas and understanding of Cuba. In her teaching, I have learned that Truth, Justice, and Liberation, in their vastness and completeness can never be held in a vessel as small and cracked as a political ideology. Their only allegiance being to Love and Healing. These are the fruits of the seeds my mother planted in me, fed by the waters of courageous and empathic honesty. Therefore, we can reject the false utopia purported by reactionary pro-capitalist white supremacy that has found a home in Cuban Miami, and the pseudo-socialist, totalitarian propaganda disseminated by current island elites and their ideological allies abroad. I use the term pseudo-socialist, because although the Cuban form of government does include several important socialist programs; a true socialist society is one that rejects the notion of a ruling and elite class, which is to say it is radically democratic, something neither Cuba, nor the US, is at this time.

Cuba libre wasn't so much the next idea I had about my mother's homeland; rather, it was an all-consuming dream and deep yearning. As a child, the only way I could describe this yearning was a profound desire for more. More for Cuba. And more para su gente. At the time, my more seemed to be nothing like the more of so many Cubanxs and non-Cubanxs. A painful lesson in understanding people's ideas of Cuba is learning frequently just how small their notions of freedom have become. For some, Cuba libre looks like the restoration of private property rights, a capitalist economy, and a racial oligarchy à la the United States. For others, Cuba libre refers to the ending of US-led hostilities, a persistence of its reputation as a romanticized revolutionary paradise, and a continuation of the current political order. And yet, still others, try to map a seeming third way towards Cuba libre, an amalgamation of the first two approximating what some call democratic socialism akin to many western European nations. This way supposedly being better because it purports a kinder, gentler version of racial capitalism.[1] No such version exists.

Counterfeit freedom, that is all capitalism, white supremacy, patriarchy, cis- and hetero-normativity, ableism, and all other systems of death have to offer. We are so starved of freedom, so desperate for libertad, that we accept these fraudulent articulations. Instead of embracing the fullness and wholeness of freedom, Cuba libre is reduced to provocations of just how much harm, domination, and exploitation we are willing to accept, and for whom. We convince ourselves that some approximated version of freedom is better than no version. We reluctantly or jubilantly accept that some change is better than none. These are the lies we tell to help the bitter medicine of compromise and resignation go down. This is how ideas of Cuba libre come to betray the very people they claim to love and cherish.

Freedom in Cuba neither began nor ended on January 1, 1959. The land now known as Cuba has not known libertad in more than five-hundred years. Not since Spanish colonizers claimed the island for their own, waged war on Indigenous communities, and forced enslaved Africans to labor for White wealth. The end of Spanish colonial rule did not bring freedom. The abolition of slavery did not bring the fullness of freedom it promised. And the overthrow of a US-backed dictatorship to only be replaced by

---

1 Cedric J. Robinson. *Black Marxism: The Making of the Black Radical Tradition, 3rd Edition*. Chapel Hill, NC: The University of North Carolina Press, 2021.

a Soviet-backed one betrayed the dream of freedom the people of Cuba held for themselves. The crushing disappointment of these historical realities leave me wondering: how do a people find themselves in a *real* Cuba libre when we've only known the nightmarish conditions of greed, corruption, domination, and violence for more than five centuries?

As I write these words, my body recalls the tension I've felt over the last twenty-five years of my life whenever I speak or write publicly about Cuba. The all too familiar waves of fear and anxiety wash over me. The fear of becoming or being perceived as an apologist for either regime before or after the 1959 revolution. The anxiety of merely being another link in the long chain of betrayal and failure to envision and actualize a true Cuba libre. Although a diasporic child of Cuba, I have rarely felt safe claiming a place in the discordant conversations, debates, and outright fights that surround Cuba and its history, image, and present reality. This ever-shifting relationship and sense of responsibility to Cuba y su gente is fueled, in part, by the rebuke I've received from Cubanx elders of my mother's generation—who I refer to collectively as "Miami Cubans"—who hear any criticism of pre-1959 Cuban society as a full-throated endorsement of the post-revolutionary political order. My deep criticisms of pre-revolutionary Cuba—with its poverty, corruption, political suppression, and economic colonization—is frequently met with anger, incredulity, and pure denial. I'm often met with rebuttals that reduce my analysis to Left-wing propaganda and dismissals relying on the fact that I was born in the US, not in Cuba, so how could I even know what things were like. Such dismissiveness stings with the air of accusation of not being Cubanx enough. And as hurtful as some of these rebukes are, I am angered more by how they reject the lived experiences and accounts of fellow Cubanxs who lived in and through the very same Cuba they did. Such rejections smack of the most corrosive form of privilege: the unwillingness to take responsibility for conditions that make revolutionary struggle and change necessary.

As a queer feminist Cubanx who has grown in my understanding and commitment to socialism and abolition, my social networks and political work have allowed me to encounter a wide variety of Left-leaning, progressive, and radical individuals and groups. I recall vividly a large gathering of progressive student activists I attended while in college where a participant in one of the breakout discussions shared with the group their deep admiration for Che Guevara, the Chilean-born revolutionary who was a central figure in the 1959 revolution and whose countenance has become synonymous with armed revolutionary struggle globally. In expressing their admiration, this student compared and likened Che Guevara to Dr. Martin Luther King, Jr. Regardless of one's opinion of either leader, to liken Guevara, a proponent of armed political struggle, with King, an avowed practitioner of non-violence philosophy and strategy, is not just historically inaccurate but dangerously cavalier.

I do not argue, nor do I believe, that armed struggle and resistance is never a justifiable tactic for achieving independence, liberation, and freedom. Violent conflict against the French in Haiti, Algeria, and Southeast Asia, the Portuguese in Angola, Guinea-Bissau, and Mozambique, and the British in Kenya, to name a few, are examples of armed liberation movements that to many, if not most, are understandable and justifiable. In my experience, what seems to get lost by many, especially those not in the armed struggle itself, are the costs of utilizing violence as a means to liberation and freedom. To be sure, non-violence has its own set of costs, and to not reckon with the consequences of how one pursues liberation and freedom runs the very real risk of romanticizing any particular strategy or effort.

Cuba, for so many progressives and radicals, remains stuck in their romanticized visions of revolutionary struggle, with little deep appreciation and understanding for the sacrifices it took to upend a social order, and even less of a critique for the state repression and domination that ultimately took hold. This shallow support of the Cuban Revolution often is less invested in the very real historical struggle of Cubanxs to be free, and instead devoted to political schadenfreude masquerading as solidarity. We, including myself, revel in the ways the Cuban Revolution and Cuba in subsequent decades has stood as both symbolic and real opposition to US power, domination, and interests. It is hard not to celebrate, at least a little bit, at any real or perceived loss to the US because the American Empire has and continues to extract with wanton disregard all over this planet. However, we must be vigilant to not let our frustration, rage, or even hatred at what the US does and does not do, lead to a systematic ignoring of injustices elsewhere. For human pain and suffering, no matter its source or where it takes place, is never justifiable, understandable, or some version of okay.

El dolor tuya es el dolor mía, el dolor de ustedes es el dolor de nosotros. I am reminded often of the need to decolonize myself of the geopolitical, social, and metaphysical borders we learn to erect to make another's misery and distress not my responsibility. Whether reactionary Miami Cubans or "well-meaning" leftists, we somehow never get to the root of the many manifestations of Cuban pain. Whether in the form of anti-Blackness, settler colonialism, homophobia, transphobia, misogyny, or state repression, el dolor de mi gente goes unmitigated because we refuse to get real. If I had to identify the one lesson I've learned in the aftermath of the 1959 revolution, I think it would be the evidence of humanity's addiction and love affair with domination and its obsession with creating hierarchies to justify it. I often wonder what change is not only possible but would necessarily transpire if we were to forego the cheap and momentary thrill of imposing our will on another.

Revolutions, independence movements, and freedom struggles are massive undertakings that are infinitely complex, mammoth in their scope, courageous in their vision and persistence, and undoubtedly fallible as any human endeavor truly is. I wish in the deepest part of my soul that the 1959 revolution was, in fact, successful, that it lived up to its hype. Held in my heart is the deepest desire that pre-revolutionary Cuban elites and their acolytes would have actually learned the lessons the Universe was trying to teach them through revolutionary deposition. Despite the fallibility of revolutions, I find myself dreaming and desiring of yet another.

This revolution toys at the edges of my imagination, enticing my mind, body, and soul with its possibilities. My ancestors whisper their consejos, explaining that *this* revolution is not the undertaking of one generation, but the fevered pursuit of many. It is a project of revolution and evolution where every successive generation is willing to unflinchingly attest to the failures of their forebears, and now knowing better do better. In this revolution there are no compromises to be made; domination in any form will find no quarter, no respite. No institution as it currently exists survives. Everything, and I mean EVERYTHING, is guided by justice, atonement, and forgiveness, which is to say everything is rooted in the very idea, practice, and energy of Love. Maybe this revolution starts in the streets, fields, waters, and hearts de mi querida Cuba, but like the air we breathe, it has no border, no boundary. This revolution is a planetary transformation.

Some will read this and accuse me of flights of fancy, of a

vision and understanding that is unmoored from reality. Such are the cancerous arguments of pessimists and pragmatists. I believe this revolution is the only pragmatic solution to the death, decay, and annihilation that capitalism, White supremacy, misogyny, and all other forms of domination beget. Our species will die, and maybe even our planet, if we don't radically and thoroughly change our path and trajectory. These are the lessons and wisdom that Cuba and its diaspora have gifted me. It is not a gift without responsibility or accountability. For every day it asks: What are you doing with every fiber of your being to make this revolution possible, doable, and unavoidable?

ABOUT THE EDITORS

David Luis Glisch-Sánchez is a healer. David is founder of Soul Support Life Coaching, their primary vehicle to live their purpose as a healer. They are a sociologist who specializes in understanding queer/trans Latinx pain. It is their work with queer/trans Latinx people that forms the basis for their healing work as a life coach. Visit www.SoulSupportLifeCoaching.com to find out more about David's practice and read more of their writing on the site's blog, Soul Corner.

Nic Rodríguez Villafañe is a nonbinary, Florida-raised, Philly-made Boricua writer, educator, scholar and DJ. For over a decade they served the community as a social justice organizer and researcher. A former Leeway Foundation Arts & Change grant recipient, their writing has been featured in an array of creative, academic, and editorial publications such as *The Philadelphia Inquirer*, *NASW Press Journal for Social Work*, and *The Gordian Review*. They are a musical collaborator and sound designer for *Eso No Tiene Nombre*, a woman-led show created and performed by award-winning poet Denice Frohman at Intercultural Journeys theatre. Nic is currently pursuing their doctoral studies in performance studies at UC San Diego's Theatre and Dance Department.

ABOUT THE CONTRIBUTORS

Christian A. Bracho is an Associate Professor of Teacher Education at the University of La Verne, and previously worked as a high school teacher and teacher trainer. His passions are teaching, learning, traveling, writing, exploring, and laughing. He dedicates his essay to his queridos papás, Leonor Gonzalez Bracho and Marco Antonio Bracho.

Claude M. Bonazzo-Romaguera received his B.S. in Applied Sociology at Southwest Texas State University in 2001 and his M.A. in Sociology at Texas State University in 2004. He completed his PhD in Sociology at The University of Texas at Austin in 2015. Claude currently teaches as a senior lecturer at Texas State University and as an adjunct Associate Professor at Austin Community College. Most recently they were appointed Director of the Latina/o/x Studies Minor.

Amaris Castillo is a journalist, writer, and the creator of Bodega Stories, a series featuring real stories from the corner store. Her writing has appeared in *La Galería Magazine*, *Spanglish Voces* and *PALABRITAS*. Her short story, "El Don," was shortlisted for the 2022 Elizabeth Nunez Caribbean-American Writers' Prize by the Brooklyn Caribbean Literary Festival. Amaris lives in Florida with her family. You can read her stories from the colmado at bodegastories.com.

Marcela Rodriguez-Campo is an interdisciplinary immigration and education community scholar. She is a formerly undocumented Colombian immigrant and first-generation college graduate. Her scholarship examines the relationship between Latinx immigrant experiences with family separation and their educational trajectories. Her work seeks to develop supportive school climates for students from historically marginalized communities. Her writings have been featured in *Childhood Geographies*, *Latinx Talk*, *Latino Book Review,* and *Huizache*. Marcela is a roller skater, gardener, and poet.

Edyka Chilomé is a queer child of migrant activists from the occupied lands of the Zacateco (Mexico) and Lenca (El Salvador) people. She was raised in migrant justice movements grounded in the tradition of spiritual activism. You can find her in the US and global South sitting at the feet of elders, recovering blood memories, and making way for a new world. Learn more about her work at Edykachilome.com.

Daniel Shank Cruz (he/they) is a queer disabled Boricua who grew up in New York City and Lancaster, Pennsylvania. He has an MFA in Creative Nonfiction from Hunter College, CUNY. Cruz is the author of Queering Mennonite Literature: Archives, Activism, and the Search for Community (Penn State University Press, 2019). Their writing has also appeared in *Crítica Hispánica, Modern Haiku, The New York Times, Your Impossible Voice*, and numerous essay collections.

Sinai Cota is the defiant daughter of Mexican immigrants, a first-generation college student and a Chicana poet who grew up in Barrio Logan (San Diego, CA). She has roots extending into Tijuana, Mexico where her family currently resides. Sinai is also author of *Pink Poems Tan Thoughts, Pan Dulce for the Latinx Soul* and *Mujeres in Movement,* a series of colorful poems and bilingual short stories that promote healing and self-love through storytelling. Sinai is also an educator and doctoral student at UC San Diego and plans to include and celebrate underrepresented student voices in higher education through her research. You can follow Sinai on Instagram @PinkChicanaPoet.

Lysz Flo is an Afro-Caribbean Latine, polyglot, spoken word artist, indie author, member of The Estuary Collective, Creatively Exposed podcast host, Voodoonauts Summer 2020 Fellow and Obsidian Black Listening 2022 Fellow. She released her poetry novel *Soliloquy of an Ice Queen* in March 2020. She is the shop owner of the online wellness shop, Crystal and Spiritual, astrolyszics.com.

Kate Foster is a poet, writer, and proud Brooklyn native. She is of Puerto Rican and Salvadorian descent. Her work has been published in *Region(es) Central magazine* Vol. II 2020 issue. As well as in *Harvard Palabritas* Spring 2020 issue. Kate's poems explore themes of spirituality, self-discovery, local and international social issues and navigates through the waters of human emotion. Her latest work can be found in the forthcoming Alebrijes Review anthology, titled *VOZ*. She is currently working on her debut collection of poetry and prose.

Cynthia Estremera Gauthier is a poet, educator, humanist, expert facilitator, and equity practitioner. She holds a B.A. and a M.A. from Penn State University and Villanova University both in English and a PhD in English and Africana Studies from Lehigh University. Cynthia has authored pieces published in blogs, journals, and edited collections. Cynthia leads regional and national racial equity and community engagement work and remains a lifelong advocate for strategies of self-care to combat white supremacist systems.

Jennifer Hernandez Lankford is an Alpha Latina seeking to spread radical self-love with her writing. After years of hiding from her true self she has chosen a journey to embrace the soul work to embody her inner Diosa. Jennifer uses her writing as a way to heal and influence other young BIPOC to do the same. As she transitions into writing more and worrying less, you can follow her on Instagram @jennthewriter.

Dafne Faviola Luna is a fat brown queer from California. She is the eldest of a small Mexican-American border dwelling migrant farm worker family. After years of therapy, she has a lovely relationship with her mom and brother rooted in body positivity and queer allyship. Her piece was written in 2017 and now in 2022 she's made a career change and lives in Virginia with her dogs Molly and Sebastian. She's a Capricorn, video gamer, and nerd.

Esperanza Luz was born in the Chihuahuan Desert and raised by a small pack of undocumented coyotes. After living in Massachusetts, Brazil, Peru, and Colorado, she returned to southern New Mexico to reconnect to the place she calls home. Today, Esperanza grows flowers and vegetables on borrowed land, plays capoeira, and continues to write, sew, and heal.

Aja Y. Martínez is Associate Professor of English at University of North Texas. Her scholarship, published nationally and internationally, makes a compelling case for counterstory as methodology through the well-established framework of critical race theory (CRT). She is the author of the award-winning book *Counterstory: The Rhetoric and Writing of Critical Race Theory*.

Ana Miramontes was born and raised in Chihuahua, Mexico. She holds a double B.A. in Theatre Performance and Media Advertising from The University of Texas at El Paso and is currently pursuing an MFA in Acting from the University of Arkansas. She has participated in the New Play Lab at the William Inge Festival, the Arkansas New Play Festival at TheaterSquared, and the Process Series in North Carolina. Actors Equity Association (EMC). https://www.anamiramontes.com/.

Daisy Muñoz is a Mexican writer and artist raised in Hawthorne, on the outskirts of the Greater Los Angeles Area. The eldest daughter of immigrant parents, she frequently addresses race, gender, mental health, and cultural identity in the US through her writing. Daisy graduated from UC Davis with a B.A. degree in History and Spanish. Her work has been featured in *Raising Mothers* and *Hispanicdotes*. She currently resides in San Francisco.

Gabriella Navas is a Puerto Rican writer hailing from Jersey City, NJ. Her work has previously appeared or is forthcoming in *[PANK]*, *GASHER*, and *Storm Cellar*. Gabriella is currently pursuing her MFA in Fiction at The Ohio State University. She is easily distracted, frequently smitten, and always willing to talk about the healing powers of Chavela Vargas's discography.

Yulissa Emilia Nunez Severino is a Dominican-American high school English teacher and amateur writer. She believes everyone has a story to share and enjoys helping people strengthen their writer's voice to do so. Yulissa also enjoys reading and holds a bachelor's degree in English from the College of the Holy Cross and a master's degree from the Middlebury Bread Loaf School of English. She dreams of living and working in the Dominican Republic with her loving cat, Luna.

Susana Victoria Parras is the daughter of Guatemalan immigrants, mother, friend, partner and a mental health therapist of color committed to generating healing, justice and care through non-carceral practices. Before she found ethnic studies, social justice, abolition, and transformative justice she found safety, hope and guidance in imperfect, spacious and loving spaces and relationships. She currently provides anticarceral mental health therapy through her practice Heal Together, building and growing Heal Together's Anti Carceral Care Collective and organizes with CAT 911 (Community Alternatives To/Community Action Teams 911) in South Central Los Angeles where she also lives, loves, and works. Susana dedicates her life to healing as a central component for justice, resistance, and activism.

Biany Pérez, (she/they) is a Bronx-born Queer Black Dominican holistic psychotherapist, intuitive coach, brujx, writer, and proud parent of three. Biany works with high achievers and survivors, both individually and in groups, guiding them on their journey to overcome self-doubt, increase self-awareness, and reconnect to their inner wisdom so that they can thrive in love and life. Check them out at www.bianyperez.com.

Sofia Quintero is a self-proclaimed Ivy League homegirl, GenX Afro-Latina author, screenwriter, and hypnotherapist. To date she has published seven books including the critically acclaimed YA novels *Efrain's Secret* and *Show and Prove* (Knopf Books for Young Readers.) Her latest YA novel is inspired by #SayHerName and will be published in 2024.

Raquel Reichard (she/her/ella) is a journalist and editor. Currently the Deputy Director of Somos, Refinery29's channel by and for Latines, her work has been published in *The New York Times, Cosmopolitan, Teen Vogue, Vibe,* and more. She has a bachelor's degree in journalism and political science from the University of Central Florida and a master's degree in Latine media studies from New York University. She currently lives in Puerto Rico's 79th municipality, Orlando, Florida.

Hector Luis Rivera has been performing poetry since 1990, inspired by the intersectional poetry, music, and political movements of the 1970s in NYC, where he grew up. You can hear Hector's poetry and song in the first two Welfare Poets' albums, *Project Blues* (2000) and *Rhymes for Treason* (2005), and in Bomba con Buya's album *Southern Sessions* (2019). Hector is the founder of Peace Inside Out, personal and community transformation through Arts, Restoration, Community, and Health.

Frankie A. Soto is a two-time winner of the Multicultural Poet of the Year award from the National Spoken Word Poetry Awards in

Chicago. *The New York Times* called his Hispanic Heritage Month performance an absolute force. He's been featured on ABC news and across the country at various universities, colleges, and high schools. His HIV poem "Guessing Game" was nominated and selected for A3C Atlanta Festival. His manuscript "Petrichor" was a semi-finalist for the 2021 Hudson Prize with Black Lawrence Press and was a finalist for the 2022 Sexton Prize with Black Spring Press in London.

Gisselle Yepes is a Puerto Rican and Colombian storyteller from the Bronx. Currently, they are an MFA candidate in poetry at Indiana University. Gisselle is a Letras Boricuas 2022 Fellowship Recipient and a 2022 Tin House Scholar. Their nonfiction piece "On Her Waters Summoning Us to Drown" won *december* magazine's 2022 Curt Johnson Prose Award in Creative Nonfiction. They are an alum of Tin House Summer Workshop, Juniper Summer Writing Institute, and Anaphora Writing Residency.

ABOUT COMMON NOTIONS

Common Notions is a publishing house and programming platform that fosters new formulations of living autonomy. We aim to circulate timely reflections, clear critiques, and inspiring strategies that amplify movements for social justice.

Our publications trace a constellation of critical and visionary meditations on the organization of freedom. By any media necessary, we seek to nourish the imagination and generalize common notions about the creation of other worlds beyond state and capital. Inspired by various traditions of autonomism and liberation—in the US and internationally, historical and emerging from contemporary movements—our publications provide resources for a collective reading of struggles past, present, and to come.

Common Notions regularly collaborates with political collectives, militant authors, radical presses, and maverick artists around the world.

www.commonnotions.org
info@commonnotions.org

BECOME A COMMON NOTIONS MONTHLY SUSTAINER

These are decisive times ripe with challenges and possibility, heartache, and beautiful inspiration. More than ever, we need timely reflections, clear critiques, and inspiring strategies that can help movements for social justice grow and transform society.

Help us amplify those words, deeds, and dreams that our liberation movements, and our worlds, so urgently need.

Movements are sustained by people like you, whose fugitive words, deeds, and dreams bend against the world of domination and exploitation.

For collective imagination, dedicated practices of love and study, and organized acts of freedom.

By any media necessary.
With your love and support.

Monthly sustainers start at $12 and $25.
commonnotions.org/sustain

MORE FROM COMMON NOTIONS

How We Stay Free: Notes on a Black Uprising
Edited by Christopher R. Rogers, Fajr Muhammad, and the Paul Robeson House & Museum

ISBN: 9781942173502 (print) ISBN: 9781942173625 (eBook)

List Price: 18.00
Format: Paperback
Size: 5.5 x 8.5
Page count: 224

Subjects: Abolition/Black Radical Tradition/Movements

In the midst of a global pandemic and a nationwide uprising sparked by the murder of George Floyd, Philadelphians took to the streets establishing mutual aid campaigns, jail support networks, bail funds, and housing encampments for their community; removed the statue of Frank Rizzo—the former mayor and face of racist policing; called for the release of all political prisoners including Mumia Abu-Jamal; and protested, marched, and agitated in all corners of the city.

How We Stay Free collects and presents reflections and testimonies, prose and poetry from those on the frontlines to take stock of where the movement started, where it stands, and where we go from here. A celebration of the organizing that sustained the uprising, How We Stay Free is a powerful collection that invites us all to celebrate Black life, find our place in an ongoing rebellion, and organize our communities for the creation of new, better, and freer worlds.

MORE FROM COMMON NOTIONS

Take Care of Your Self: The Art and Cultures of Care and Liberation
Sundus Abdul Hadi

ISBN: 9781942173182 (print)
ISBN: 9781942173403 (eBook)

List Price: $16.00
Format: Paperback
Size: 8x5
Page Count: 144

Subjects: Art/Self-Care/
Decolonization

"Take care of yourself. How many times a week do we hear or say these words? If we all took the time to care for ourselves, how much stronger would we be? More importantly, how much stronger would our communities be?"

In *Take Care of Your Self*, Sundus Abdul Hadi turns a critical and inventive eye to the notion of care and how it relates to social justice. In contrast to the billion-dollar industry of self-care, Abdul Hadi identifies care as a necessary practice—rooted in self, community, and the world—in the collective process of decolonization, empowerment, and liberation.

Abdul Hadi explores the role of art in building regenerative narratives to confront and undo systemic oppression and trauma. Weaving in the work of visionary transcultural artists who engage the liberatory intersections of struggle and care, Abdul Hadi centers the voices of those most-often relegated to the margins and emphasizes the importance of creating brave spaces for their stories and art. The transformative power of care exists in these spaces, building a foundation for a world in desperate need of healing and change.

MORE FROM COMMON NOTIONS

For Health Autonomy: Horizons of Care Beyond Austerity—Reflections from Greece
Edited by CareNotes Collective

ISBN: 9781942173144 (print) ISBN: 9781942173359 (eBook)

List Price: 15.00
Format: Paperback
Size: 5 x 7
Page count: 144

Subjects: Health / Mental Health / Social Movements

The present way of life is a war against our bodies. Nearly everywhere, we are caught in a crumbling health system that furthers our misery and subordination to the structural violence of capital and a state that only intensifies our general precarity. Can we build the capacity and necessary infrastructure to heal ourselves and transform the societal conditions that continue to mentally and physically harm us?

Amidst the perpetual crises of capitalism is a careful resistance—organized by medical professionals and community members, students and workers, citizens and migrants. *For Health Autonomy: Horizons of Care Beyond Austerity—Reflections from Greece* explores the landscape of care spaces coordinated by autonomous collectives in Greece. These projects operate in fierce resistance to austerity, state violence and abandonment, and the neoliberal structure of the healthcare industry that are failing people.

For Health Autonomy is a powerful collection of first-hand accounts of those who join together to build new possibilities of care and develop concrete alternatives based on the collective ability of communities and care workers to replace our dependency on police and prisons.